The Transcultural Leader, Leading the Way to PCA (Purposeful Cooperative Action)

Leadership for All Human Systems

DR. JONATHAN E. SMITH

Copyright © 2013 Dr. Jonathan E. Smith.

All rights reserved. No part of this book may be used or reproduced by any means, graphic, electronic, or mechanical, including photocopying, recording, taping or by any information storage retrieval system without the written permission of the publisher except in the case of brief quotations embodied in critical articles and reviews.

WestBow Press books may be ordered through booksellers or by contacting:

*WestBow Press
A Division of Thomas Nelson
1663 Liberty Drive
Bloomington, IN 47403
www.westbowpress.com
1-(866) 928-1240*

Because of the dynamic nature of the Internet, any web addresses or links contained in this book may have changed since publication and may no longer be valid. The views expressed in this work are solely those of the author and do not necessarily reflect the views of the publisher, and the publisher hereby disclaims any responsibility for them.

Any people depicted in stock imagery provided by Thinkstock are models, and such images are being used for illustrative purposes only.

Certain stock imagery © Thinkstock.

*ISBN: 978-1-4497-9843-7 (sc)
ISBN: 978-1-4497-9844-4 (e)*

Library of Congress Control Number: 2013910745

Printed in the United States of America.

WestBow Press rev. date: 06/13/2013

Table of Contents

Chapter 1: Trans-Cultural . . . to be or not to be 1
Language of Trans-culturalism
Background: Providing the Backdrop for This Study
Theoretical Overview of Leadership
    The Leader-Follower Relationship
    Bogus Empowerment
    Charisma and Its Limitations
    Transactional and Transformational Leadership
    Bass's Position
The Trans-Cultural Leader
    Trans-Cultural Journey Towards Leadership
    Characteristics of a Trans-Cultural Leader
        Situational Strengths
        Synthesis of Characteristics

Chapter 2: Culture Understood 35
Universality of Culture
Subjective Culture
Synthesis of Triandis's View of Subjective Culture
Organizational Culture

Chapter 3: Creating through Dialogue 51
Dialogue: The Road Toward Connection and Collaboration
Buber and Bohm
    Martin Buber (1878-1965)
    David Bohm
    Types of Dialogue
    Application of Dialogue

Chapter 4: Trans-cultural Leadership Undergirded Culture, Life Journey, and Dialogue..... 87

Understanding of Culture Applied
Life's Journey
Dialogue Utilized
Heart/Mind/Soul of Trans-Cultural Leadership
Heart/Mind/Soul in Action

Chapter 5: Putting it all together 123

Analysis of Characteristics
Journey Towards Understanding
Culminiation of the Trans-cultural leader
The Heart of Trans-cultural Leadership
The Mind of Trans-cultural Leadership
The Soul of Trans-cultural Leadership

Chapter 6: Trans-Cultural Leader in Light of the Literature.. 137

Questions asked and answered
Implications of This Book

Conclusion 149
About the Author... 151
References 153

Tables

Table 1: Characteristics of a Trans-Cultural Leader
Table 2: The Heart, the Mind, and the Soul Framework
Table 3: Trans-Cultural leader's Heart, Mind, and Soul

Figures

Figure 1: Continuous Flow of Relationship with God, Self, and Others in Racially/Culturally Inclusive Faith Community
Figure 2: Levels of Trans-cultural Leadership concerning organizational culture
Figure 3: Characteristics of a Trans-cultural Leader
Figure 4: Steps Towards Evolving Culture
Figure 5: Brining the Many to One as a Trans-Cultural Leader
Figure 6: Connection to the Supreme Other Facilitating Connection w/others
Figure 7: Disconnection from the Supreme Other Creating Disconnection from others
Figure 8: Summing up Bohmian Dialogue
Figure 9: Flow of Generative Dialogue to Strategic Dialogue and Back Again

I

Trans-Cultural . . . to be or not to be

One may ask . . . What is it to be Trans-cultural? Being trans-cultural is to purposely interact with people by transcending cultures' natural barriers with the sole objective of bringing the "many" to one in vision, purpose, and action. You too may be wondering what Purposeful Cooperative Action (PCA) is and why is it important? Well . . . Purposeful Cooperative Action (PCA) is the deliberate movement towards a common goal and shared vision by people of different groups, professions, races, and/or disciplines. The thought of people with differences working together towards a common goal seems surreal in this time of global political, financial, and social unrest. But, now more than ever is the time to "hold hands", sing "We Are the World", and move towards togetherness! I wish it were that simple! The phrase "Purposeful Cooperative Action (PCA)" denotes hard work, for surely to be purposeful requires deliberateness and intense focus of energy while resisting the increasing urge to succumb to the mental and physical fatigue brought on by the process of deciding to authentically address the issues at hand. Cooperation insists that the parties involved jointly focus on the issues at hand and thereby willingly compromise while ignoring the urge to reject and not consider the "others" and their opinions. Cooperation also brings with it the understanding that to move in unison is to be "other" focused and not "the child of your mother" focused; not insisting on always having "your" way completely. PCA asks people to deliberately set aside some of their perceived needs and wants in order to move in unison towards a common goal. Some people find it difficult to operate in that fashion and would benefit from a leader that is able to co-create the environment of inclusion conducive for PCA. The Trans-Cultural leader, the leader of the 21st century, is the type of leader well equipped for the job; one who has an understanding of his/her leadership journey and the cultures in which they interact and able to create a place where dialogue abounds.

The leader of today has to be able to lead in a way that will energize and mobilize those in which s/he wishes to lead. The 21st century calls for leaders to unlearn, learn and re-learn ways to interact with others within their spear of influence. People of today approach life differently than they did just 20 years ago, which brings with it different expectations for their leaders. The authoritarian leader of our parents' and grandparents' time has gone the way of the tyrannosaurus rexes.

This century is an exciting time in which to live; it is a time when conversations about global markets, global villages, and global communities are becoming more prevalent. Borders that separate countries, cultures, and people have become increasingly more porous during this new century. The world is connected now more than it has ever been. Evidence of the world's consecutiveness can be seen in many different phenomena, ranging from this current global economic downturn to the seeming ease at which deadly viruses spread around the world. In times past, natural barriers and distances would keep ideas, cultures, and even viruses from reaching far beyond their own regions. We, as a global community, are indeed connected.

Perhaps the most exciting thing resulting from this era of global connection is the increased interaction between people of different cultures in communities and organizations. This is indeed the best of times; yet, it can be the worst of times. It is the best of times because the possibilities are endless for those who are able to ride the waves of cultural diversity and connection. It can be the worst of times when there is no effort on behalf of leaders to utilize the innate power of diversity and connection. This time in history affords us the opportunity to create environments of inclusion in organizations and communities that respect and celebrate the differences that exist amongst us. Then communities and organizations will be able to come together, discover common purpose, and move toward cooperative action. In his inaugural address, U.S. President Barack Obama spoke about transcending differences, uniting, and creating an inclusive world. He used the word "patchwork" to describe this country's heritage and pointed out that our heritage is our strength not our weakness. (Obama, 2009, p. 4) The President's use of the word *patchwork* brings to mind a patchwork quilt with all its pieces threaded together, each piece maintaining its uniqueness. Such an analogy is quite fitting in describing this nation, its people, and its many cultures. Although Obama was not speaking about organizational cultures, it is my belief that the underlying sentiment is applicable to ethnic, national, and organizational cultures alike.

An interesting occurrence that results from the increased interactions between people of different cultures is more awareness of their differences and uniqueness. Awareness of this led me to two consider two possibilities: First, in the midst of diversity, people may tend to seek out what is familiar, comfortable, and like themselves in as many ways as possible. Second, there may be a need for leaders in many venues to understand the natural human tendency to belong to their groups and withdraw from other groups, and these leaders should able to lead above the barriers made by people attempting to maintain their uniqueness.

The natural human tendency to belong and be a part of a group is described in Maslow's (1943) hierarchy of needs. Maslow's hierarchy of needs has influenced management theory for years (Hofstede & Hofstede, 2005). The theory posits that a person has a set of basic human needs that form a hierarchy. In this theory, physiological needs such as safety and security must be met before love, belonging, self-esteem, and self-actualization. The need of love and belonging fuels the human's longing for a place of acceptance and affiliation. Consequently, Murray (1938) listed affiliation among 20 basic human needs.

People are social creatures and endeavor to be a part of groups, to join clubs, and to be accepted by others. That endeavor covers every aspect of our human existence. Wubbolding (1988) wrote that the needs for belonging are manifested in society, work, and family. An observer of people can easily find groups in all three of these categories. For example, there are Christians and Muslims, management and staff, and the Hatfields and the McCoys.

Once people form their groups and experience belonging, they may feel compelled to defend and protect their groups, especially if something is interpreted as threatening. In this instance, defending is not defending to the point of being separatist but defending in an attempt to preserve the group in the light of an increasingly diverse world and workplace. In *Affirming Diversity, the Sociopolitical Context of Multicultural Education*, Nieto (2000) explained the aforementioned phenomena as occurring when people develop pride in their culture and begin to feel conflict while living in a society where language appears to be assimilationist. The use by leaders of phrases such as *melting pot* has the connotation that different cultures are thrown together, melted down to their most basic elements, and somehow made into something completely new, with few of the characteristics of the contributors. Therein lays the conflict; perhaps groups, and the individuals who comprise them, seek only to survive, to be healthy, and to grow. Thus, the apparent assimilationist language and perceived assimilationist environment places the group in a defensive or a survival mode, which further highlights the differences between the different groups.

Differences are complex and can appear to be insurmountable as we try to navigate in a world of contrary ideals, beliefs, and ways of doing business. The complexity can cause tension among all those involved. Trompenaars and Hampden-Turner (2004) described the complexity of this world as "nonstop culture clashes" (p. 230). These authors explained that when they wrote about culture they were referring not only to nations but also to different professions, genders, etc. In every venue, there needs to be those who are able to lead regardless of the cultural clashes and boundaries facilitated by the natural human tendency to form and preserve groups.

How can a leader lead above and across the manmade boundaries of culture brought on by the human need to belong and help them become one in purpose, in vision, and in action? Isaacs (1999) wrote about the comments of a Syrian astronaut as he was orbiting the earth. The astronaut commented on how beautiful the earth appeared to be with all the boundaries apparently gone. Of course, the boundaries were still there, but the astronaut's stellar view allowed him to transcend the manmade boundaries, and, instead of seeing individual countries, he saw the beauty of one world that holds many different people. Leaders of the 21st century need to have such a stellar view in order to transcend the cultural boundaries put in place by people in attempts to preserve their groups' uniqueness.

The transcendent type of leader is needed in all aspects of society, from the community to the corporation. Though the concepts put forward in this book could be applied to many different venues, the focus of this discussion will be organizational cultures. Trompenaars and Hampden-Turner (2001) provided an excellent reason for the need of trans-cultural leadership in corporations when they wrote, "Business cultures are different, so different as to be in some respects diametrically opposed, and that, because business is run differently around the globe, we need different managerial and leadership competencies" (p.11). The competency Trompenaars and Hampden-Turner wrote about involves the leader having the ability to navigate through situations that could potentially block the inclusive process. In their book titled *21 Leaders for the 21st Century*, these authors put forward the opinion that trans-cultural leaders must have the ability to recognize, respect, and reconcile differences in order to successfully lead in the 21st century.

Perhaps it takes leaders who are able to draw on the attributes given them by their respective groups. Leaders influenced by Western society may approach this phenomenon differently than those with an Eastern influence. Consequently, Lewis (1996/2006) wrote that Western leaders must depend on dynamic leadership, insightfulness, psychological skills, a willingness to innovate, and clever use of their democratic institutions to lead people of different cultures.

The people of the United States, according to Simons, Vázquez, and Harris (1993), have the benefit of being recipients of some of the world's most ambitious and capable immigrants. If there is no understanding of how to lead such ambitious and capable groups of people, we as a society will never reach our fullest potential. Hamel (2007), in his book titled *The Future of Management*, wrote that the very things that make us great as a people are what will allow us to become leaders who are able to coordinate the efforts of many individuals without strangling human imagination and allow freedom and discipline to flow in tandem.

This book is based on information gathered from a phenomenological study where I examined the experiences of four trans-cultural leaders from various fields who lead people of different races, genders, professions, and/or disciplines towards purposeful cooperative action. Exploring the experiences of trans-cultural leaders from different fields provided insights into and best practices used to create inclusive environments that promote cooperative action.

Language of Trans-Culturalism

An intricate part of culture is language. Language can be a barrier to understanding and cooperation; therefore, I will provide the reader with definitions of the terms used throughout this study.

Culture: There are many definitions of culture. Negandhi (1983) has even argued that it is virtually impossible to define such a dynamic concept. Hofstede and Hofstede (2005) defined culture as a collective phenomenon in which the human mind is programmed to be able to distinguish one group from another. Just as in Hofstedes' definition, the word *group* is used to define culture, and I, too, will use the word *group* to refer to culture throughout this book. Hereafter, culture will be defined as the evolutionary manifestation of people's experiences and interactions with the challenges and difficulties presented by their shared time periods, environments, vocations, and situations, of which the people build assumptions that determine their groups' behaviors.

Boundaries: This term is used in Family Systems Therapy and is defined as "the emotional barriers that protect and enhance the integrity of individuals, subsystems, [cultures] and families" (Corey, 1996, p. 393). For the purposes of this study, I have added the word *culture* to this definition provided by Corey.

Trans-cultural leader: Trans-cultural as defined by Simons et al. (1993) is being knowledgeable of one's own culture yet having general and specific cultural skills to be able to work, live, and interact in a multicultural environment. However, Simons et al. also suggested that there is not just one blueprint of the trans-cultural leader. Brown (2007) defined a trans-cultural leader as someone who is perceptive of national and cultural differences and does not profess to know everything about the unfamiliar culture in which he or she works. A combination of these definitions will provide the reader with a good understanding of the type of leader spoken of in this book. For the purpose of this book, a trans-cultural leader will be defined as a person who has positive influence over several different groups of people operating within the same organization or community and who utilizes his or her understanding of culture to create an inclusive environment conducive to transcending the manmade boundaries of culture and facilitating purposeful cooperative action.

The word *person* was chosen in the above definition because leadership is predicated not on position or title but on relationships and influence (Maxwell, 2005). In *The 360º Leader, Developing Your Influence From Anywhere in the Organization,* Maxwell posited that a person could lead from any position in an organization as long as he or she has a followership. The foundation of the 360º leader's effectiveness is the level of influence the leader has and uses. The concepts reveled in this book should be applicable to any person who has influence over a group of people in a multicultural environment. Therefore, for the purpose of this book, the phrase *trans-cultural leader* applies to leaders at all levels who fit the definition.

Cultural cohorting: A cohort can be defined as a group of people unified to perform one goal or purpose. Therefore, for the purpose of this book, cultural cohorting is defined as the act of different cultures uniting to perform one goal or purpose.

Purposeful cooperative action: Purposeful cooperative action is defined as the deliberate movement toward a common goal and shared vision by people or groups of different races, genders, professions, and/or disciplines.

Human Activity System: Bela H. Banathy, (1992) wrote that a human activity system is a set of activities carried out by a group of people to fulfill a certain purpose. Therefore, a human activity system can be anything from a family, church, or business.

An understanding of the definitions provided above will prove to be very handy on one's journey towards PCA. The journey will require the reader to consider the backdrop of the book in conjunction with gaining an understanding of leadership foundations, culture and dialogue.

Background: Providing the Backdrop for This Book

Throughout this book, I will share the challenges of culture and seek to show how trans-cultural leadership transcends manmade boundaries of culture. The following section is intended to provide the reader with the backdrop for this book. First, I will discuss a qualitative study conducted in 2006. Second, I will discuss a consulting experience I had working for a multidisciplined service organization in New Orleans and Baton Rouge, Louisiana. These two experiences led me to seek greater understanding of the phenomena of trans-cultural leadership.

A phenomenological researcher utilizes a literary style that helps the reader see the phenomena clearly. A part of helping the reader see the phenomena clearly is accomplished by providing a backdrop for the book and the phenomena being discussed. The backdrop delineated here will help the reader understand what lead me to take this experiential journey.

My personal journey towards understanding trans-cultural leadership started a several years ago during a research practicum class. My qualitative study (Smith, 2006) explored the life-giving factors of Lighthouse Covenant Fellowship Church, which was a multicultural church in the San Francisco Bay Area when it was functioning at its best. The research attempted to understand and explain six parishioners' experiences as members of this multicultural faith-based organization.

The research showed that the parishioners of this church placed utmost importance on their relationship with God and believed it greatly affected their views of themselves. The parishioners believed their closeness to God allowed them to know themselves in deeper ways.

I observed that the self-awareness brought on by a close relationship with God allowed the parishioners to form deep, meaningful relationships with others. The meaningful relationships that were formed became the platform for the development of meaningful multicultural relationships. Upon analysis of the parishioners' responses during the interviews, it was evident that the factors that combined to make Lighthouse Covenant Fellowship Church the multicultural church it was were the parishioners' relationships and behaviors. These relationships and behaviors were as follows: (a) relationship/fellowship with God (outer "greater than I" focus); (b) increased self-awareness; (c) purposeful action with other focus; (d) relationship/fellowship with others; (e) multicultural relationship—building; (f) conversation about race/culture with repentance and forgiveness; (g) formation of a culturally inclusive faith community; and (h) corporate purposeful action with other focus, which was driven by the leadership's purposeful creation of a culturally inclusive environment (see Figure 1).

The Transcultural Leader, Leading the Way to PCA

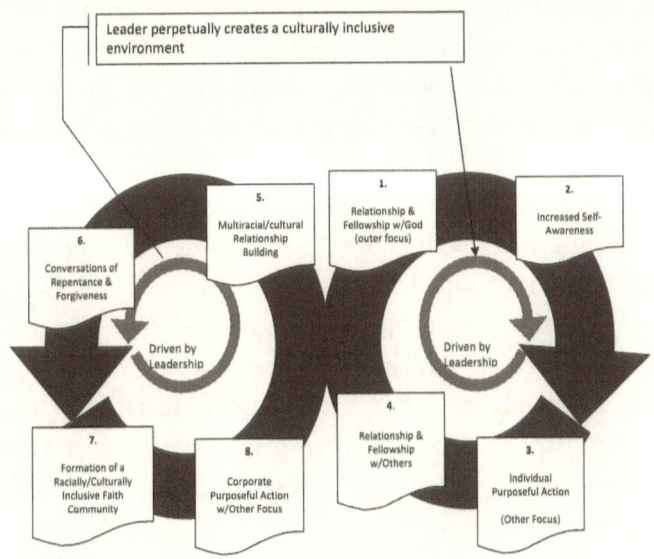

The leader's influence appeared to me at the time to be the catalyst that moved the organization toward cooperative action because he was purposeful in creating a culturally inclusive environment. He made a concerted effort to have a culturally diverse ministerial leadership team in order to reflect the congregation. The leader also deliberately chose music that was "middle of the road" in order to reach a larger population. "Middle of the road" was a phrase used by the original leader to explain his deliberate choice to use worship music that did not fit one specific genre (i.e., too much of an R&B sound or too much of a country sound). He also delivered messages that had poignant delivery but did not follow one cultural tradition.

Shortly after the completion of the study, the leader accepted a promotion and was subsequently replaced. The new leader was a very well-intentioned leader; however, he appeared to lack the trans-cultural leadership abilities of the previous leader. The church slowly changed to a predominantly African-American church and lost its multicultural attributes. Members started to leave Lighthouse Covenant Fellowship Church to attend churches that were more "comfortable" for them. It appeared that the church leadership was not being purposeful when it came to developing relationships with and between its parishioners, even though the current leadership claimed to pursue multiculturalism. It is unfortunate that leaders often give diversity lip service and do not place much emphasis on building a culturally diverse environment (Klie, 2007).

Another part of my journey toward understanding trans-cultural leadership was a consulting job I had in Baton Rouge and New Orleans, Louisiana. The owner of Smith Research Corporation (SRC) asked me to come to Louisiana because the management could not agree about anything and did not appear to have a purpose. One could focus on the negative factors that could be contributing to this problem, but the owner and I decided to approach the project using Appreciative Inquiry (AI). I have found that going through the AI questioning process as a group and analyzing the emergent themes together allows participants to realize that they have fertile common ground on which they can connect. AI encouraged the managers and leaders to value the best of SRC. In contrast, a problem-solving approach focuses on what needs to be fixed, and the underlying language is deficit based. While there is a place for problem-solving, it is not conducive to helping groups realize their common and life-giving purpose.

The management team of SRC consisted of 12 members from five different departments of the New Orleans office. This project identified the essence of the participants' experiences in the organization. I believed that AI was the best approach for this particular project because it allowed participants to build relationships and to heal wounds that they may have acquired during their working journeys together. Healing is achieved during the interview process by the telling and retelling of positive life changing stories. Whitney and Trosten-Bloom (2003) posited, "Appreciative Inquiry can also be used in a wide variety of ways to enrich spiritual development, heal wounds among diverse groups, and enhance personal relationships" (p. 30). The project ended with the leadership of SRC combining their efforts as individuals and departments and moving toward the goal of serving the individuals of New Orleans by providing high quality maintenance in a timely manner through caring and responsive service.

Mr. Smith, President/CEO of SRC, was the driving force behind the process of leading people of different cultures, races, and disciplines to one in purpose, vision, and action. Mr. Smith moved his company from a small minority-owned, majority African-American business to a successful multicultural support services business fulfilling multimillion-dollar contracts for the federal government at various locations throughout the country.

My intention to understand the makeup of such a trans-cultural leader is the driving force behind this book. Explaining the experiences of trans-cultural leaders while they lead diverse groups of people toward purposeful cooperative action holds the potential to add to the understanding of the intricateness of effective leadership that transcends the manmade boundaries of culture.

Theoretical Overview of Leadership

Understanding the characteristics of a leader that leads people with differences towards purposeful cooperative action necessitates addressing the topics of ethics in leadership, the leader-follower relationship, empowerment, and types of leadership. This section ends with a comparison of transactional and transformational leadership, which provides the reader with a good platform from which to launch into the world of the trans-cultural leader.

Can leadership be labeled as "good" or "bad"? There are many views on this topic. Ciulla (1998) believes ethics should be embedded in leadership, and she rephrases the question of what is leadership to what is good leadership. According to Ciulla, a leader exhibits goodness in two ways: One way refers to technical goodness as in being good at the job, and the second way is related to being morally competent. For one to lead without having a sense of ethics is to lead haphazardly without any concern for morality. Leadership without ethics at its core holds the potential to facilitate leadership through corrosion, manipulation, or trickery. To be "good" and a leader is to set the foundation for establishing trust between the leader and the follower and to ensure that one is leading in a way that benefits the greater good and not just the organization or a few people.

The leader-follower relationship. A leader cannot lead without followers. There should be a symbiotic relationship that exists between the two, for they both should help the other, as opposed to a parasitical relationship where only one benefits. The perfect example of a symbiotic relationship would be the relationship between my wife and our unborn children. My wife's body fed them the vital nutrients needed for their growth and development. She also protected our children from harm by providing them with a home inside her body. Our children provided my wife with several things. She reported that her hair grew longer, her fingernails grew longer and stronger, her skin appeared to look better, etc. the mother's improved appearance could be a result of her improved immune system, which typically accompanies pregnancy. My wife was clearly the one with the power in the relationship, as she could have chosen to not eat properly, to drink alcohol, to smoke cigarettes, or to not follow up with her prenatal care, or even to not allow the forming embryos to take up residence in her body for 9 months. Because of her overwhelming joy at the thought of being a mother and her self-perception that she could be and is a good mother, the relationship between my wife and our children still grows and flourishes to this day. Our children all agree that they have a great mother, including our 23—year-old son! Her greatness is evidenced by their abilities to confidently navigate through our children's life challenges and developmental stages. The mother provides the child with her body, love, and nurturance, and the child provides the mother with unconditional love and acceptance, which could be seen as a symbiotic relationship.

Followers' perceptions of the leader are, in part, determined by the leader's self-perception projection. A leader who is aloof and appears to be dishonest or power hungry is not contributing to a positive leader-follower relationship; therefore, the way a leader presents him or herself affects the way the follower follows. Ciulla (1998) wrote about the "social contract" that exists between the leader and the follower. In this contract, because the leader has more responsibility, more benefits are given. Unfortunately, the leader who seeks the benefits without the responsibility of creating a safe environment, where the followers feel that they are co-laborers with the leader, will never attain the true camaraderie needed to be successful.

Bogus empowerment. Ciulla (1998) used the term *bogus empowerment* to describe what happens when leaders seek the benefits of leadership without the responsibility and make promises to the followers; this allows the leaders to feel that they are co-laborers endowed with certain powers, but in all actuality they have less power than they thought or no power at all. Good leadership is based on honesty; therefore, when the leader appears to be honest, the followership readily places their trust in that person. The bogus-empowered leader attempts to control the follower with the appearance of "niceness" in order to achieve the wanted goal, but, sadly, this type of leader never intended to share power, and the follower eventually discovers this and becomes dissatisfied. Bogus empowerment is detrimental to the organization's health and may stunt the organization's growth. On the other hand, companies that allow employees to have real power could do much better than those led by leaders using bogus empowerment.

Charisma and its limitations. Charisma seems to be something not fully understood by many scholars of leadership. What appears to be commonplace in the understanding of charismatic leadership is the ability of the leader to tap into the emotions of followers and achieve a level of trust within those followers. Solomon (1998) wrote that charismatic leadership is based on the emotional relationship between the leader and the follower coupled with trust. The author also pointed out that emotionalism can be dismissed in business realms. If that is the case, leadership seeking to downplay emotional attachment could be problematic because people are emotional beings. Leading in the business realms without appealing to followers' emotions would not allow the follower to completely "show up" on the job.

This country's churches are full of "charismatic" leaders, or those trying to exhibit charismatic qualities. It appears that the charismatic leader draws on the emotional needs of a group of people by passionately pursuing goals or visions projected by the leader. The movement of the organization is fueled by the leader's ability to generate trust and to passionately project a vision that resonates powerfully with the followership. A limitation of such leadership is that movement is centered on the leader, the vision, and the trust the leader has earned. Thus, if the trust is lost for whatever reason or the passion has diminished and/or the vision no longer resonates with the followership, movement may be greatly hindered. Charisma could be a component of good leadership, but it cannot be the sole component.

Transactional and transformational leadership. Transactional leadership is leadership in which the leader offers incentives to encourage cooperation on behalf of the followers. This type of leadership satisfies the "right now" purposes of the organization as well as individual purposes of the followers. The transactional leader seeks to provide the lower-level needs on Maslow's (1943) hierarchy of needs scale in order to enable the followership to perform a particular task at a particular time.

Transformational leadership seeks to help the followers look beyond their personal needs and focus on a "higher good." The transformational leader leads the followers in a common goal, of which charisma plays a part, whereas an emotional bond is formed between the leader and the led. Ciulla (1998) mentioned James MacGregor Burn's theory of transformational leadership and pointed out that his theory clearly drew on Maslow's (1943) hierarchy of needs. Burns (1978) believed that a transformational leader must operate at a higher level of needs, thereby turning the followers into leaders. This type of leadership sees the big picture and concentrates on long-term goal completion, not short-term fixes.

Bass's position. Bass (1998) believes that gains achieved by transactional leadership are significantly small when compared to gains achieved by transformational leadership. A leader who has morally uplifting values would be defined as a transformational leader and a leader who is lacking the morally uplifting foundation would be defined as a peudotransformational. Bass (1998) wrote that peudotransformational leadership is the type of leadership the opponents (Keeley, 1998) of transformational leadership speak of when they claim that transformational leadership is unethical. Transformational leadership focuses the awareness of the followers to what is right and good and leads the followers away from self-interests to being concerned with the common good. According to Bass, this type of leader does not lie about situations because trust lies at the heart of transformational leadership. However, it may be necessary for a transformational leader to give troubling information in a nonabrasive way in order to keep hope alive in the organization.

The Trans-cultural leader promotes morally uplifting values and seeks to help his/her followers focus on the "higher good" while simultaneously encourages self and other awareness.

The Trans-Cultural Leader

This section provides the trans-cultural perspective of leadership and leadership development, followed by a definition of a trans-cultural leader. I then present characteristics of trans-cultural leaders, followed by a synthesis of such leaders' characteristics.

I liken the trans-cultural leader to the fluent reader. I taught elementary and middle school for 4 years, and I noticed the progression of aspiring readers. There are several stages of readers. The first stage of a reader is the emergent reader. The emergent reader understands the direction of the text and knows the sounds of the alphabet but has a very hard time putting it all together and reading fluently. The second stage of reading is the early reader, who enjoys reading as long as the reading is not too difficult; decoding skills are developing as demonstrated by the child's ability to read the text more fluently with few mistakes. In the third stage, the fluent reader decodes so quickly that he or she does not seem to think about it—he or she just reads. The fluent reader enjoys reading and looks for opportunities to use his or her skills.

I believe the progression towards trans-cultural leadership can be characterized in similar ways (see Figure 2). The lowest skilled-level leader in cultural awareness is the *oblivious leader*, one who knows very little about multicultural issues and is not concerned with learning about issues pertaining to organizational culture. This type of leader is concerned only with giving orders and the bottom line. The *conscientious leader* is one who has learned little about multicultural issues as they apply to organizational culture, and sees the benefits of applying these issues but does not know how to. The *multicultural leader* is one who has learned much about multicultural issues from reading, classes, seminars, and many other learning sources but has difficulty transferring the learned information into practice. This type of leader sees the importance of multicultural leadership but clumsily applies the concepts. The *trans-cultural leader* has a firm grasp of multicultural leadership and has no difficulty in leading people from different cultures. He or she applies the concepts naturally, apparently with little or no effort.

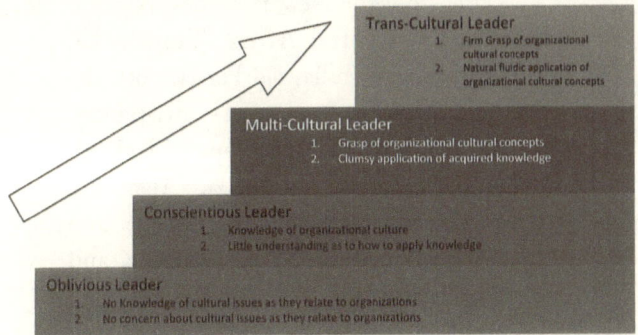

Figure 2. Levels of Trans-Cultural leadership concerning organizational culture

Trans-cultural journey towards leadership. This section examines leadership from a trans-cultural perspective. Stech (2009), in his article titled "A Trans-Cultural Perspective on Leadership and Leadership Development," wrote that theories and models of leadership generally rise in the western world; this is unfortunate because there are so many other traditions upon which one could draw. To remedy that, Stech's paper focused mainly on the work of Campbell (1990), who studied mythologies from a plethora of cultures and posited that the overarching themes found in these stories about heroes and heroines provide the reader with a trans-cultural view of leadership and leadership development. Stech's rationale for presenting Campbell's work was that "there is a body of knowledge in comparative mythology that extends across cultures and also spans the history of humankind from prehistory into more recent times" (p. 21). Campbell's research studied myths from across the world. The stories

> ... came from the New Hebrides, Nigeria, East Africa, Central Africa, Tanganyika, Egypt, Sumeria, India, old Persia, both the Old and New Testament of Christianity, Russia, Finland, China, Japan, Ireland, England, Denmark, Canada, Australia, Melanesia, ancient Rome and Greece, and the Native American Navajo, Apache, and Algonquin people. (Stech, 2009, p. 21)

These cultures all had striking similarities concerning their treatment of heroes or heroines, which Campbell believed mirrors these cultures' views of leadership. According the Campbell, the hero takes a journey towards his or her life's call. The hero's journey starts at home where he or she receives a "call" to service, which he or she cannot truly answer without help rendered from a source "beyond friends, family and peers" (p. 69).

After accepting the call, the hero goes through several stages. Stech (2009) quoted Campbell (1990) and described the stages as follows:

> In the stage of "trials and victories of initiation," there are a series of trials represented by dangers and crises.... Having survived trials [the hero then] attained simplicity, resisted temptations, and become a partner with the great authority figure, the next step is apotheosis, reaching a special state, a feeling of transcendence, peace, and enlightenment ... the hero becomes part of the universal and timeless, "at one" with whatever basic principle might exist in the universe. (p. 22)

According to Campbell, after the "trials and victories of initiation stage" (p. 22), the hero then returns and reintegrates into his or her society with purpose and vision. "Re-crossing the threshold can be painful; it is a movement from the realm of visions and dreams, of ideas, to the land of human needs, conflicts, and limitations" (Stech, 2009, p. 21). The hero is now a master of both worlds and able to go back and forth as the situation dictates.

Stech (2009) stated that a study of the myths of other cultures suggests that the journey's result produces leaders, which is vastly different from the common idea of leadership and leadership training, where the leader is taught how to become a leader. Conventional leadership training can teach "appropriate behavior or critical skill . . . in that sense, results in people who are able to 'act' as leaders" (p. 23). Stech expanded this concept by stating that conventional leadership training could impose constraints on the leader because he or she denies himself or herself in order to conform to the concepts presented that could be foreign to his or her culture of origin. The leader must be true to the culture from which he or she came, while recognizing and valuing the cultures they lead. Only then can the leader lead trans-culturally and "lead without conscious effort" (p. 23).

Characteristics of a trans-cultural leader. In a previous paper I wrote titled *Leading across Human Barriers: the Many to One Purpose* (Smith, 2008), I presented the possible characteristics of a trans-cultural leader. I will rely on the concepts developed in that paper to support this part of our discussion.

Having the ability to lead across cultures is essential in a world where cultural boundaries abound. Homogeneous boards and groups can become myopic; thus, corporations must actively seek to become more culturally diverse (Hoffman & Hendrickson, 2006). For a leader, understanding diversity is a foundational skill because as the world's boundaries become more and more porous, leaders are called to still lead with relevance and effectiveness (Green and Berthoud, 2007). Organizational Development finds its roots embedded deep in the concepts of inclusion (Katz & Miller, 2007), whereas interest in trans-cultural leadership is a natural occurrence for the OD professional. Furthermore, trans-cultural management research has been influenced by several different social sciences (Negandhi, 1983). The reason for this influence phenomenon could be attributed to the nature of the subject being researched, which is the human being. Hofstede (2003) defined management as being "always about people, getting things done through other people; or more specifically, coordinating the efforts of people towards common goals" (p. 30). Studying management, then, draws from the fields that study people and their interactions with each other and their environments.

The trans-cultural leader should be an astute observer of the human experience. An understanding of the "purposefulness" of human behavior will provide the level of insight required for leading in multicultural communities or organizational environments.

Kane-Urrabazo (2006) wrote, "While managers do not deny the importance of organizational culture ... few fail to realize the direct impact they have in shaping it" (p. 188). It is believed by some that the head controls the direction the body goes; the head in this case would be the leader. During my years as a high school and collegiate athlete, linebacker coaches would tell me, "Keep your head up!", because if I were to let my head drop down, down I would surely go. Wherever my head went, the rest of me would follow. Perhaps the same holds true for leadership. If the leader chooses to move toward inclusion, the group will follow. Fontaine (2007) stated that cross-cultural management is about perspectives, and we must seek to understand perspectives that will allow all those involved to know from where each other is coming. In order to understand human behavior in specific situations, one must be able to see actions in context. Asking for an explanation of circumstances that caused specific actions by certain people has the potential to provide the context needed to understand others' experiences.

Good leaders are seldom one-dimensional people; they are often very confident, assertive, deliberate, humble, patent, and principled (Gandz, 2007). Even though the ideas put forth by Gandz may be true, there is little theory about the types of leadership behavior needed to be effective in various organizations (Masoond, Dani, Burn, and Blackhouse, 2006). However, there could be similar traits shared by successful leaders.

A trans-cultural leader should understand that culture is an action verb, a point brought forward by Grillo (2005), who implied that in order to work with culture, one must be willing to go into action—to actively seek to understand culture, its charteristics, its movements, its "changeability." A trans-cultural leader must be an astute observer of culture. Schein (1996) wrote," To discover the basic elements of a culture, one must either observe behavior for a very long time or get directly at the underlying values and assumptions that drive the perceptions and thoughts of the group members" (p. 11).

Such leaders should be "principled." Seijts and Kilgour (2007) defined principled leaders as ones who determine what their values are as well as the values of organizations, and abide by them consistently. They are considerate of others around them and are not hostile towards the people within their sphere of influence.

Maxwell (2006), in his article titled "Lead Others by Learning to Lead Yourself," encouraged leaders to make the right assumptions about people by understanding that people want to feel worthwhile, encouraged, and motivated. Thinking this way about subordinates would greatly increase a leader's chances of facilitating change and creating an environment to ask the right questions in order to challenge the undesired assumptions. Giving the right assistance by taking time to work with subordinates through tough problems is another trait that would help the leader to lead trans-culturally.

Situational strengths. A trans-cultural leader should be able to consider situational strengths while leading. Masoond et al. (2006) believe situations may be the most ambiguous aspect of leadership, and situations can affect the leadership process. The authors divided situations into two categories: strong situations construe the situation in the same way and draw the same conclusions. The situation is the catalyst and determinant of the appropriate responses. A good example would be the public's response to a stop sign. All of us, for the most part, know that the sign means to stop a vehicle, which is the appropriate response. A weak situation is where there is ambiguity about the meaning of the situation, and the appropriate response or the individual response may be different. Masoond et al. suggested that a trans-cultural leader would be more effective in dealing with the latter situation, possibly because the strong situational strength-oriented culture would, by its very nature, be very resistant to change. However, a trans-cultural leader should be an agent of change, whether the road is difficult or easy.

It is critical for the leader to grasp the role of corporate cultures because it is culture that moves us (Trompenaars and Hampden-Turner, 2004). Before a leader can be a change agent in his or her organization, that leader must first earn the right to be heard. Maxwell (2005) wrote that a leader's position gives him or her the right to speak, but the leader must earn the right to be heard. Maxwell's right to be heard is akin to Hill's (1992) earning subordinates' respect. Caley (2007), in his article titled "Including All Points of View," posited that mentoring is very important and that the leader must guide the process.

To create an environment of inclusiveness, a leader must overcome his or her self-deception and bias. Becoming self-aware and understanding one's own prejudices and previously hidden biases can be very difficult. A person can do this by initiating conversations about developing a culturally inclusive environment. Leaders are the ones to help subordinates beyond the obstacles that might hinder the inclusion process. Coffey and Tombari (2005) also posited the need to identify and eliminate hurdles that arise during the process of creating diverse organizational cultures. The leader must commit to continuous learning and improvement and promote communication and education. Triandis (2006) believes that leaders must be culturally intelligent and stated that the most important contributor to cultural intelligence is suspending judgment until enough information becomes available. Triandis wrote that suspending judgment allows people to collect information without making judgments. The leader succeeds by looking for current behavior in different situations; identifying what information is relevant for making judgments; integrating information in order to make a correct judgment; overcoming "ethnocentrism," a mindset that holds a belief that the leader's own culture is the best and most correct culture; and placing oneself in the shoes of members of the other culture. The transcultural leader must be able to suspend judgment, observe current group behavior, identify relevant information, and overcome ethnocentrism.

Table 1 lists the characteristics of a trans-cultural leader gathered from a variety of authors.

Table 1

Characteristics of a Trans-Cultural Leader

Author(s)	Characteristics
Resick, Hanges, Dickson & Mitchelson (2006)	<ul><li>Considers relevant moral issues</li><li>Mindful of the consequences his or her decisions have on all parties involved</li><li>Concerned with the common good</li><li>Ability to motivate others</li><li>Places group interests above his or her own</li><li>Promotes independent thinking in subordinates.</li></ul>
Seijts & Kilgour (2007)	<ul><li>Principled</li><li>Reflective</li><li>Ethical</li><li>A model citizen</li><li>Culturally aware</li><li>Facilitates the free flow of information</li></ul>
Kane-Urrabazo (2006) D'Avirro (2007)	<ul><li>Trustworthy</li><li>Ethical</li><li>Empowers others</li><li>Delegates appropriately</li><li>Mentors subordinates</li><li>Community minded</li></ul>
Maxwell (2006)	<ul><li>Understands subordinates' needs to feel worthwhile, encouraged, and motivated.</li></ul>
Masoond et al. (2006)	<ul><li>Makes appropriate decisions in strong or weak situations.</li></ul>
Hill (1992)	<ul><li>Competent</li><li>Transparent</li><li>Relational</li></ul>
Bond (2003)	<ul><li>Culturally open</li><li>Accommodating</li><li>Humanizing</li><li>Legitimizing</li></ul>
Miller, Fields, Kumar, & Ortiz (2000)	<ul><li>Good sense of humor</li><li>Sincere interest in subordinates</li><li>Culturally competent</li></ul>
Swanson (2004)	<ul><li>Able to expand perspective, explore options, and create alternatives</li></ul>
Coffey & Tombari (2005)	<ul><li>Able to identify and eliminate hindrances to cultural inclusion</li></ul>
Triandis (2006)	<ul><li>Able to suspend judgment, observe current group behavior, identify relevant information, and overcome ethnocentrism</li></ul>

Synthesis of characteristics. Despite extensive research in the field, the characteristics of a trans-cultural leader are still elusive. Hence, I agree with Masoond et al. (2006) that "there is little theory or evidence concerning the kinds of leader behavior required in various organizational settings" (p. 194). The quest to find the characteristics of a trans-cultural leader has been quite challenging; however, compilation of the information cited in Table 1 provided me with the foundation upon which to build. I have compiled the attributes mentioned above from the various resources of this section and placed them in three different groups—the Heart, the Mind, and the Soul. I choose these groups because they speak to the areas into which leadership must tap in order to be truly trans-cultural.

For the purposes of this book, the Heart is defined as the part of leaders that allows them to connect with themselves and others. They draw on their life experiences—where they grew up, how many siblings they have, and the amount or type of challenges they may have had. A result of drawing on life experiences allows leaders to be humble, not in a "doormat" kind of way, but in a "but-by-the-grace-of-God-there-go-I" kind of way. These leaders are not conceited. Having keen insight is another attribute of trans-cultural leaders. They are self-aware and able to draw on the inner feelings they may have concerning certain situations. They are able to be reflective in their thinking process and consider the whole situation. Lastly, they are very confident and have feelings of self-assurance.

Regarding the Mind, trans-cultural leaders are very astute observers, with keen discernment when it comes to their surroundings. They are analytical in their approach to their work and their lives. These leaders analyze situations and seek to understand as much as they can about the situation at hand. Their actions are very deliberate because they have carefully thought through their responses. Workers readily follow them because they have demonstrated that they are competent in their positions.

The Soul is the part of trans-cultural leaders that guides them and allows them to guide others through organizational life. They are patient with themselves, their peers, and their subordinates. They provide the space needed to allow others to perform at their best. These leaders are very principled when it comes to life in the organizational world and the private world. They live with honor and command respect from all those around them not because of their position but because they are seen by all as trustworthy persons.

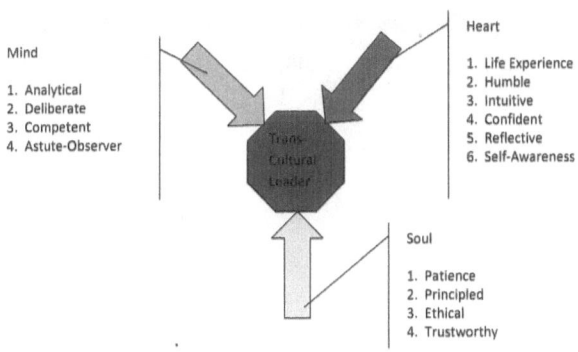

Figure 3. Characteristics of a trans-cultural leader

The characteristics of trans-cultural leaders mentioned above are not all inclusive. I believe that a trans-cultural leader would not necessarily have every point under each heading. But a developing leader could use the information provided in Table 1 to move to higher levels of being trans-cultural as he or she is conscious of the Heart, the Mind, and the Soul.

Could a person lead with only a few of the characteristics previously presented? It is probable. However, the evolutionary process of becoming such a leader gives way to the idea that there could possibly be developmental progression; however, it is not the intention of this book to develop the schema for such a process.

As mentioned above, the trans-cultural leader must be an "astute observer of culture." To become such an observer, one must have a working definition as to what culture is and how it applies to his or her current situation. The following section is intended to set the stage for developing a working definition of culture. I use the phrase *working definition* because culture is an evolving phenomena; thus, the definition should be one that is able to evolve also. I will also present the concept of subjective culture.

II

Culture Understood

Thomas and Inkson (2003) insisted that knowledge of culture is the first place to start when seeking to become culturally intelligent. They defined cultural intelligence as

> . . . being skilled and flexible about understanding a culture, learning more about it from your ongoing interactions with it, and gradually reshaping your thinking to be more sympathetic to the culture and your behavior to be more skilled and appropriate when interacting with others from the culture. (p. 14)

Thomas and Inkson likened a culturally intelligent person to the ancient Greek Proteus, as he could change shape and become whatever he needed to be in any particular situation because of his knowledge of the situation. The trans-cultural leader's understanding of culture further strengthens his or her credibility in facilitating cultural inclusion and change. Like Proteus, the trans-cultural leader can use awareness of differences to shape and meet the trans-cultural context demanded of this unique approach to leadership.

Christie, Kwon, Stoeberl, and Baumhart (2003) commented in their article "A Cross-Cultural Comparison of Ethical Attitudes of Business Managers: Inida, Korea, and the United States,"

> Culture is a loaded and complex variable. It is an abstraction. It is too simplistic to consider culture as one single independent variable and associate differences or similarities in ethical attitudes with it. Culture needs to be unpacked into a set of interpretable components (cultural dimensions) and these cultural dimensions would better serve as an independent variable than cultures taken as a whole, to arrive at valid conclusions. (p. 16)

Negandhi (1983) suggested that culture is one of those things that defy a single definition and that there are as many definitions as there are people who use them. I believe, however, that even though there are several ways to describe culture, there are common bonds that tie groups together and several principles that could assist in the process of inclusion.

In this journey toward a deeper understanding of the human experience as it applies to how people work in groups toward a shared goal, one has to develop a working definition of culture. The word *culture* is, indeed, a complex concept, and it means different things to different people. When some think of culture, they think about brown—and-white issues, but one can move toward more of an encompassing definition with the realization that culture does not apply to just color. The above quote is correct in that it is "too simplistic to consider culture as one independent variable" (Christie et al., 2003, p. 16). Culture encompasses all that influences the behavior and mental life of a particular group of people.

Culture reflects the human experience and, therefore, there must be some commonalities on which to build. Hall (1977/1989), in his book *Beyond Culture*, wrote,

> Everything man is and does is modified by learning and is therefore malleable. But once learned, these behavioral patterns, these habitual responses, these ways of interacting gradually sink below the surface of the mind and, like the admiral of a submerged fleet, control from the depths. (p. 44)

Even though each submarine may have differences and be made by different groups of people from different parts of the world and different companies, they all must function under the same natural laws, which are present no matter what ocean in which they operate.

Worldviews are created as cultures evolve because of the interactions between people and groups of people. Nieto (2000) provided several dimensions to her definition of culture, and she includes social and political relationships, worldviews, language, social class, and religion. Nieto's definition gives culture a transformative quality in that all the dimensions listed in her definition are transformed by a group of people bound together by several external factors. Sue and Sue (2003) defined culture as being a culmination of all those things that people have learned in their history that informs their actions, beliefs, skills, tools and customs.

Schein (1996) posited that culture is a set of assumptions about how the world should be and is shared by a group of people. Schein's (2004) definition evolved in his book *Organizational Culture and Leadership*, where he added that behaviors of the group, if they worked well enough, would be considered valid and taught to newcomers. Schein (1996) stated, "Culture arises through shared experiences of success" (p. 12). The following simplified illustration was adapted from Schein's (1996) paper and shows the evolution of culture.

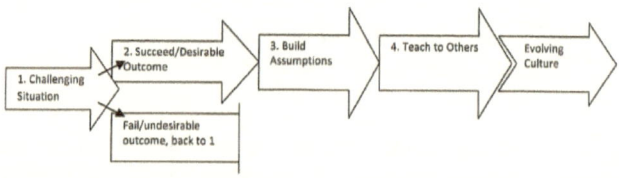

Figure 4. Steps toward evolving culture

Schein's (2004) definition shows the change and growth potential of cultures; it also leaves space for connection between cultures. The "challenging situation" could refer to a gambit of issues, which can be similar to the issues experienced by another group of people and which in turn could lead to a sharing of common ground necessary for inclusion.

Hofstede and Hofstede (2005) wrote that culture is a phenomenon that is shared by people who live within the same social environment. Culture is specific to groups of people and can be learned and taught to others, but it is different from human nature and personality. Human nature is that which is common among all humans (i.e., the more "base" feelings such as fear, anger, love, and happiness). Personality is more of a specific and unique attribute of the individual, which is influenced by genetics and life experiences. The Hofstedes listed four levels of culture in their book—*symbols, heroes, rituals,* and *values.* Symbols are those things that are most superficial and that easily change. Heroes are people—alive, dead, or fictional—who embody the ideals of the culture. Rituals are the collective activities that are carried out for the purpose of reinforcing the group dynamic. Symbols, heroes, and rituals are all things that can be observed by the outside world; the authors labeled these as practices. Lastly, values are things that are not so readily seen by the outsider but are made up of things that are learned throughout the life of the participants of the culture. Values are a system of preferences, where something is preferred over its alternative.

Schein's (2004) levels of culture—artifacts, espoused beliefs, and values, and underlying assumptions—overlap, to some extent, with the Hofstede and Hofstede's (2005) levels. Schein's first and second tiers—artifacts, espoused beliefs, and values—are the things that are seen by people outside and newcomers to the culture, which are characterized as practices by the Hofstedes. The deepest of Schein's levels—underlying assumptions—is a stabilizing factor for the culture and will be defended vigorously. Peterson (2004) wrote that culture is a relatively stable set of values and beliefs held by groups of people. It is interesting that Peterson's choice to use the phrase *relatively stable* substantiates the description of culture by Hofstede and Hofstede and by Schein. It appears that in order to change a culture, one would have to challenge the stabilizing factor.

Negandhi's (1983) assertion was that culture is one of those things that defy a single definition and that there are as many definitions as there are people who use them. Keeping this in mind, I define culture as the evolutionary manifestation of a group's shared experiences and interactions with the challenges and difficulties presented by their shared time periods, environments, vocations, and situations, from which the group builds assumptions that determine the behaviors of its members.

Evolutionary manifestations, I believe, allow for a group's adaptation to the shared problems as they change. Like in nature, a group must be able to evolve with its surroundings and realize that changing situations call for changing assumptions. A group of people could be individuals who have different life experiences and even belong to an additional group based on different experiences; however, that does not exclude individuals from "membership" within his or her work culture, faith culture, race culture, gender culture, or any other forum where people join together. Williams (2007) wrote,

> In the context of social exchange, culture can be thought of as an institution in much the same way markets and firms are

institutions—including culture, markets, and organizations . . . by extension, culture, which can be viewed as a type of institutional form, is the behavioral outcome of a repeated game in which individuals develop beliefs and strategies based on the incentive structure of social life. (p. 250)

Not all situations are the same, but the people within those situations are more similar than not. Therefore, it stands to reason that a definition of culture would be broad enough to be applied to the commonness of the human experience but specific enough to be applied to the minute details of the various combinations of groups' dynamics in relation to the inexhaustible supply of situations.

A good understanding of culture allows the observer to ask the right questions in the quest to learn about a specific culture. Questions concerning the origin of the group, including the peoples' thoughts as to what aspects of their environments, time periods, vocations, or situations presented problems to the group and how they overcame, help the observer develop a deeper understanding of the group's dynamics. Also, the observer could find what assumptions about the outcomes direct their behavior.

Universality of culture. Christie et al. (2003) expressed that culture is too complex to define because so many factors influence its development. Schein (2004) and Hofstede and Hofstede (2005) provided readers with levels of culture that can be applied to its understanding in a universal sense. Peterson's (2004) assertion that culture has within its core a set of values and beliefs held by people lends itself to the idea that similarities between cultures exist. Even when the values and beliefs appear to be vastly different, the human element in culture will provide some similarities on which groups can build. One example of the similarities could be the general belief that life is valuable and should be respected. It is my belief that culture is indeed a complex concept and can be difficult to define in a way that will encompass its vastness. However, culture, as seen through the lenses of Schein, Hofstede and Hofstede, and Peterson can be defined by drawing on the similarities within the human experience.

Subjective culture. Williams (2007) pointed out that cultures can be seen as institutions like markets and organizations. These institutions can be studied because they are visible and very alive. A good way to observe such institutions is to listen to their language.

Triandis (2003) wrote about the subjective culture, and he suggested that people in each culture have certain ways of looking at "human-made" parts of the environment, which include such concepts as ideas, theories, politics and religion. An understanding of subjective culture would allow the observer of cultures and the potential facilitator of the cultural cohorting process to move toward purposeful cooperative action. Triandis started with language. He suggested that a way to analyze subjective culture is to identify terms that do not have an equivalent in other cultures; this would shed light on how people of a certain culture categorize experiences. Cultures in the process of their evolution develop ways of communicating and being that may be unique to that particular culture, and, to develop an environment for connection, one must attempt to understand the language. Once a category is discovered, it is important to "discuss" the categories with members of the culture being studied in order to draw a greater level of understanding from the member's category. This process facilitates dialogue between culture groups and individuals within the groups.

One thing that will arise during the process of discussing the differences of the cultural language is the recognition of stereotypes. Triandis (2003) wrote that stereotypes can be used to highlight cultural differences. He listed two types of stereotypes: autostereotypes, which reflects the group's view of itself, and heterosterotypes, which is a reflection of how a group sees the other. Understanding these types of stereotypes in relation to cultural cohorting allows the leader to gauge the degree of differences between the groups. An understanding of how members of a group see themselves in relation to their world, in addition to seeing how they see the other, and visa-versa, could shed much light on the behavior of the groups. This concept proved to be very useful in understanding how the New Orleans group interacted with each other. Members of the New Orleans group saw themselves as expendable, and they felt very insecure because of the temporary nature of their jobs. The owner's observation that the management could not agree about anything and that they did not appear to have a purpose can be better understood in light of Triandis's formula.

Triandis (2003) presented a formula he found to be important to understanding subjective culture: "The probability of an act is a function of behavioral intentions

(I) and habits (H), multiplied by facilitating conditions (F). P = (I + H) F" (p. 15). Triandis posited that a group's actions are a combination of intentional behaviors plus the deep-seated assumptions, which he called habits, multiplied by what group members think about themselves and the environment in which the group operates. Triandis subsequently wrote, "This theory has been too complex to test in its entirety. In the future, as our technology develops and permits tests of such theories, it might be tested" (p. 15).

Synthesis of Triandis's view of subjective culture. Triandis' (2003) view of subjective culture is beneficial to the quest of understanding culture and how cultures may interact because it prompts the observer to consider how group members look at themselves and others in relation to the environment in which the group exists. Triandis also wrote about perceived similarity and how he believed it is a key construct in dealing with diversity in the workplace because when people see the similarities between each other, the "culture shock" is limited. The greater the perceived differences, the greater the "culture shock."

Triandis's (2003) formula helps an observer of culture better understand the behavior of a culture. For example, at SRC, the probability of an act (development of a hostile and highly competitive working environment) is a function of behavioral intentions (management's desire to make its section the project's "stellar" section) and habits (self-preservation—looking out for "number one"), multiplied by facilitating conditions (pressure from corporate office and the Federal Emergency Management Agency to serve the community of New Orleans quickly and efficiently). The owner of SRC made the statement, "The management can't agree about anything and they don't have a purpose," and can be better understood in light of Triandis's formula. The leaders rarely agreed because they were in constant competition. The leaders chose to fight amongst themselves and vie for position instead of joining together in the face of shared difficulties. The owner saw this pattern and sought to change it. The ability to see hindrances to cultural inclusion is an asset to the trans-cultural leader.

A trans-cultural leader's understanding of culture should be broad enough to be applied to the commonness of human experiences and specific enough to be applied to the minute details found within human experiences.

One must also consider how people in a culture see themselves in relation to their environment and other cultures. This process includes listening to the language spoken by people of different cultures (i.e., what words a specific people group uses to describe a challenging situation) and how they overcame or failed within a particular situation. The observer of culture can then compare the languages of the two different cultures and find similarities that would help bring the many to one. The trans-cultural leader understands that bringing the many to one is the best route toward strength and vitality.

Trans-cultural leaders are able to lead across human-made cultural boundaries because they have an understanding of culture and are able to allow their understanding to evolve or change completely, depending on the information they have at the time. An understanding that culture is the evolutionary manifestation of group members' shared experiences and interactions with the challenges and difficulties presented by their shared time periods, environments, vocations, and situations, of which the group builds assumptions that determine their behaviors, is a good place to start when working with culture. Trans-cultural leaders actively seek cultural understanding and are astute observers of the human experience.

Organizational Culture is different from ethnic cultures in the respect that people choose to be a part of that particular organizational culture and could leave it at any time. However, to understand a person's behavior within the organization, one must understand the person's culture of origin, which is underneath and driving the behavior. Moreover, being a culturally astute observer of cultures is an important part of leading an organization trans-culturally. Also, being aware of one's own culture and understanding the cultural traits that may influence one's interactions with followers is just as important to the trans-cultural leader. Hofstede and Hofstede (2005) posited that a leader leads according to the culture into which he or she was born. The leader is a part of the national societies within his or her culture, and, in order to understand another culture, the leader has to understand those societies.

One of Hofstede and Hofstede's (2005) interesting observations is "power distance," in which dependant relationships play a major role. Power distance is the degree to which the subordinate within a society accepts the unequal distribution of power. Small power distance societies tend to have a limited dependence of subordinates on bosses, and large power distance societies tend to have more dependence of subordinates on bosses. Hofstede and Hofstede wrote that examples of power distance can be seen in most interpersonal relationships—such as relationships between parent and child, between teacher and student, and even between boss and subordinate—because such institutions are a mirror of the parent society. The Hofstedes then presented the idea that the attitudes people place on their parents and teachers can be transferred to their bosses.

Hofstede and Hofstede (2005) also presented the idea of individualism and collectivism in societies. Individualist societies have loose ties between individuals, and collectivist societies have very strong ties between individuals. In the individualist society, a person is expected to "find his or her own way." Looking out for oneself appears to be prevalent in such societies. The collectivist society, on the other hand, encourages a person to operate in groups and to be loyal to the collective. Relationships at work are undesirable and discouraged in individualist societies, but collectivist societies are built on strong relationships and are seen as a natural occurrence in the organizational realms.

According to Hofstede and Hofstede (2005), societies can also be categorized as masculine and feminine as well, which can occur in individuals, families, peer groups and organizations. Gender roles learned in the family are continued in peer groups and organizations. Hofstede and Hofstede explained that societies are termed masculine when the men are deemed to be the hunter, the protector, the decision-maker, and the accumulator of material goods (i.e., house, car, food) and when the women are deemed to be docile, soft, and the gentle maker of the nurturing environment. Conversely, a society is termed feminine when the gender roles overlap and both genders exhibit the "softer" qualities previously mentioned.

Another factor alluded to by Hofstede and Hofstede (2005) is uncertainty avoidance, which addresses the human need to avoid things that are vague and unclear. Drawing from the work of March and Olsen (1976), Hofstede and Hofstede pointed out that many people do not like "not knowing," and, just as people come up with ways to avoid the anxiety bought on by not knowing what will take place, societies and cultures do the same. Some societies, as some people, have a laissez-faire attitude concerning the unknown—the "whatever-will-be-will-be" kind of approach—while others implement quite stringent ways of decreasing the level of anxiety felt by society members as a whole by attempting to control their environments. There are different gradations and combinations of each within persons, groups, and organizations.

Hofstede and Hofstede (2005) wrote that in the workplace uncertainty avoiding organizations have more laws and informal rules controlling the rights and duties of employers and employees. People in these economic societies have been programmed to feel comfortable in structured environments. Countries with weak uncertainty avoidance believe that rules should be implemented only when really necessary. When considering Hofstede and Hofstede's views on culture and organizations, a trans-cultural leader should remember that people react according to their "mental programming," which affects people's views about organizations. It behooves trans-cultural leaders to understand their programming in relation to the programming of their followers and to react accordingly because motivation plays a big role in leading, and different cultures are not motivated by the same conditions.

Hofstede and Hofstede's (2005) presentation on culture and organization appears to be more global in its scope and application, which would provide the trans-cultural leader a good road map for leading in different cultural contexts. Understanding the mental programming of the individual within the organization could help the leader assist a new employee in learning various nuances of the work culture in relation to mental programming as that person adds his or her uniqueness to the collective. The process of learning about the variety of cultures that one may encounter in the workforce is the same, fundamentally, as the process of getting to know neighbors of other cultures and creating a neighborhood that goes through life's situations and struggles together. A key component to the cultural cohorting experience is the wiliness to communicate.

III

Creating through Dialogue

An integral part of the human experience is the exchange of ideas through communication. The effective trans-cultural leader must be able to create an environment conducive to the free exchange of ideas without fear of reprisal or reprimand. Such an environment can do nothing but strengthen an organization. The following section looks at dialogue as an effective way to include all those involved in the movement toward purposeful cooperative action.

The open and free exchange of ideas is necessary for PCA to occur. Trans-cultural leaders should be able to facilitate and participate in the ongoing dialogue between the different cultures within the sphere of her/his influence.

Defining dialogue is not as simple as one might think. When I mentioned my intention to write about dialogue to one of my peers, her response was, "What! Everyone knows how to talk!" Some people have oversimplified the concept of dialogue and assumed it is something we all do naturally without coaching (Yankelovich, 1999).

Dr. Jonathan E. Smith

The likelihood is that dialogue has interested people since humankind learned to speak. The concept is dealt with in early religious writings, as well as in Greek philosophy. For example, in Isaiah 1:8, NKJV, *"'Come now, and let us reason together,' says the Lord"* was written as a response to an obvious conflict of worldviews. The people of that time lived under a theocratic government in that they believed that they received their civic and social direction from the God of the universe. The writer of this ancient text, believed to be Isaiah, saw that his countrymen were living contrary to the laws they received from God (i.e., doing good, seeking justice, rebuking oppressors, defending the fatherless, and pleading for the widows; Isaiah 1:17, NKJV). Because they were not doing such things, two opposing views emerged—to live according to God's law or to live according to man's ways.

The words *reason together* in the above passage are derived from the Hebrew word *Yākhach*, which means to dispute with someone, to argue, to mediate, or to arbitrate. (Zodhiates, 1994). Ballantyne (2004) posited,

> Reasoning together can descend into a dialectical contest between adversaries, in which case shared meaning can be lost in the combat . . . dialogue is certainly not an adversarial form of communication, nor another manipulative communication technique for transferring messages and meaning. (p. 117)

But reasoning together spoken of in the holy text is drawn out from a continuous relationship to dialogue. It is not intended to be "combat" (for who can fight with God and win?) but is instead intended to create a place where decisions can be made and options considered. The writer of Isaiah, here, is asking for a decision to be made between beings that have had a history of generative dialogue and now focus is required. Their dialogue now becomes strategic. Generative and strategic dialogue will be discussed later.

In ancient Greek philosophy, the meaning of the words *reason together* is more descriptive, where it is used as a noun *logos*, which denotes the "inward" thought itself, a reckoning, a regard, a reason (Vine, Unger, & White, 1980/1985). It is also used as a verb *dialogizomai*, which means to bring together different reasons and reckon them, and *dialegomai*, which means to think through one's own differences in thought and to ponder them to dispute with others. Finally, *suzēteō*, which means to seek or examine together, is another application of the phrase (Vine et al., 1980/1985).

It is interesting and encouraging that Isaiah's faith system allowed for dialogue between his countrymen, and even between God and his countrymen. The idea of sitting down and openly sharing differences with the hope of creating positive outcomes may well be timeless. However, the process can be very involved and time consuming, requiring actively listening, purposefully recognizing the other, and truly considering the other to the point that a sincere attempt is made to see things from all possible perspectives.

There is a sense of sacredness when it comes to dialogue, in that we deal with our innermost concerns, fears, joys, desires, and pains as we attempt to consider the other. We tend to resist the idea of having our assumptions challenged, or we resist the idea of working hard to expand our thoughts by possibly integrating other points of view into our own. It is so much easier for us to state our opinion and say to ourselves, "Either they take it or leave it," because we are not willing to invest the time and effort needed to participate in the dialogic process.

People of antiquity understood the importance of dialogic interactions, but we in this age have, for the most part, left this ageless process behind. A return to the Holy Scriptures reveals a directive to the adherents of the Christian faith to "be ready to give a defense to everyone who asks you a reason for the hope that is in you" (1 Peter 3:15, NKJV). The heart of this directive is dialogue! The sacred life is lived and expressed through dialogue. Buber (1947/2002) wrote, "If that is religion then it is just everything, simply all that is lived in its possibility of dialogue. Here is space also for religion's highest forms" (p. 17). On the other hand, Isaacs (1999) wrote that the problem is that people are not able to recognize the undercurrents of conversations. Dialogue occurs during deep-level interactions, which most people of today are not willing to have with each other. With regard to dialogue, Bohm (1996) wrote, "I think the whole human race knew this for a million years; and then in five thousand years of civilization we have lost it, because our societies got too big to carry it out" (p. 16). I have observed that, as communities, we grow so big and move so fast in order to maintain the hustle and bustle of modern life that we forget how to sit and share the meaning of our various experiences with others.

Isaacs (1999) provided a modern definition of dialogue as "a shared inquiry, a way of thinking and reflecting together" (p. 9). He added that dialogue is not something you do *to* others but something you do *with* others. Isaacs stated that the word *dialogue* comes from "the Greek words *dia* and *logos*. *Dia* means 'through'; *logos* translates to 'word' or 'meaning.' In essence, a dialogue is a *flow of meaning*" (p. 19). Dialogue is a quest for collective meaning (Bohm, 1996). Senge, Kleiner, Roberts, Ross, and Smith (1994) wrote that dialogue helps people think togeather, "not just analyzing a shared problem or creating new pieces of shared knowledge, but in the sense of occupying a collective sensibility" (p. 358).

Dialogue: The road toward connection and collaboration. Collective sensibility provided by dialogue has the capabilily of moving through all aspects of the human experience. Dr. Martin Luther King understood that the desire to create community resides in humans. We long to be connected to others. In order to maintian the connection, we must collaborate. King (1963/1986), in his defense of integration delivered in Nashville, Tennessee, said,

> At the heart of all that civilization has meant and developed is "community"—the mutually cooperative and voluntary venture of man to assume a semblance of responsibility for his brother . . . . Man could not have survived without the impulse which makes him the societal creature he is . . . . I cannot reach fulfillment without thou. (p. 122)

Dr. Jonathan E. Smith

I, as a holder of a theology degree, believe King's (1963/1986) reference to the *I* and the *thou* points to the dialogic principles presented by Buber (1970), which will be discussed later. King was an accomplished theologian and would have been exposed to Buberian thought, as is the case in most theological seminaries. At a time when the country is fractured by misunderstandings, fear, and hate, King called us to "turn" toward each other and connect.

It is a given that we—humankind—cannot survive without connection with others. "The WE includes those elements of the mind pertaining to the deep desire to be connected to others and with the underlying belief that one is connected to them" (Newman & Newman, 1975/1999, p. 336). Connecting is being present with another being, sharing meaning without requiring agreement, but only seeking to understand what is, and by deliberately and purposefully interacting between the "I" and the "YOU." Deliberate and purposeful interaction occurs when the parties concerned spend time familiarizing themselves with the other, whether the other is a group of people or a person. This interaction allows the participants to move toward a level of familiarity that makes dialogue possible, which, in turn, holds the potential to lead to collaboration. Collaboration allows the "I" and the "YOU" to join together for cooperative action (the "WE").

The Transcultural Leader, Leading the Way to PCA

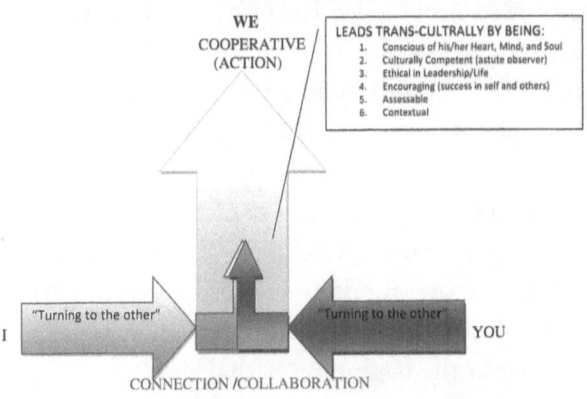

Figure 5. Bringing the many to one as a Trans-Cultural Leader

Buber and Bohm. Before connecting and collaborating, the "I" and the "YOU" must turn towards each other. The concept of turning is presented by Buber (1970) in his book titled *I and Thou*. An understanding of the Buberian concept of "turning" provides trans-cultural leaders with a very important tool they can use in their quest to create a culture of dialogue. When the participants of dialogue turn toward each other, they encounter obstacles that could prevent true connection, obstacles such as succumbing to the urge to defend certain views and the inability to suspend reactions. Bohm's work on dialogue provides the trans-cultural leader with a "guidebook" useful for overcoming obstacles to dialogue. The following sections present Buberian and Bohmian dialogic principles.

Martin Buber (1878-1965). Buber was a poet, a novelist, and a translator of the Torah (Hebrew Bible), and he provided key insights on dialogue in his seminal work titled *I and Thou*. Kramer (2003) wrote that Buber was born in Vienna and studied philosophy in several universities. According to Kramer, "Martin Buber's *I and Thou* is about practicing as well as understanding genuine dialogue—our 'human birthright'" (p. 12).

Buber's (1970) description of the encounter between two beings is characterized as the "I and Thou" relationship or, for a more modern rendering, the "I and You" relationship. He speaks of the actual "turning towards" the other as the beginning of dialogue.

Turning is the first step in the dialogic process. People bound together in dialogue must turn to one another (Buber, 1947/2002). Buber (1947/2002) defined the space that is created when two beings turn toward each other as sacred. He believed that one cannot adequately connect to the other without connecting to God. Buber (1947/2002) called this interaction the *above and below*. His section on above and below shows that a connection with the other is hindered if there is not a connection with the "supreme other." A person must understand his or her place in relation to God in order to connect with the other. One must appreciate the sacredness Buber ascribed to dialogue. His emphasis on the "supreme other" shows that we, in order to achieve deeper meaning between ourselves, must first reach outward to that which is "higher than I" (Psalms 61:2). Kramer (2003) pointed out, "Thou is not restricted to a person; it includes "animals, aesthetic objects, nature, inspired forms, and God" (p. 43). Buber's above-and-below belief shows the importance of the interactions between the creatures below. "A newly-created concrete reality has been in our arms; we answer for it. A dog has looked at you, you answer for its glance; a child has clutched your hand, you answer for its touch; a host of men moves about you, you answer for their need" (Buber, 1947/2002, p. 20). We live in dialogue; we just have to answer its call.

Buber (1970) placed a high priority on dialogue when he wrote, "'I'" does not exist without You . . . my You acts on me as I act on it" (p. 67). The very act of turning towards another is a metamorphic occurrence. The other changes from something looked at but not seen to something actually gazed upon with the desire to encounter the world and share meaning together. Buber noted, "When I confront a human being as my You and speak the basic word I-You to him, then he is no thing among things nor does he consist of things" (p. 59). At that point each person becomes something more and different to the other.

Buber (1970) explained this by using "It" and "You" when referring to the other. He created a wonderful picture in the minds of the reader when he equated the "It" with a chrysalis and the "You" with a butterfly. According to Buber (1970), the "I" causes the "It" to morph into a "You" when the "I" turns toward it. The picture of the chrysalis changing into a butterfly denotes process, in that no butterfly changes overnight. The act of turning starts the process, and the continuous act of engagement moves the process. The engagement is what creates the beautiful butterfly. As "I" turns toward "It", "It" morphs into a "You"; as "I" turns away from "You", "You" morphs into an "It."

Turning does not necessarily require language. Human dialogue is more than "sound and gesture." Buber

Dr. Jonathan E. Smith

(1947/2002) posited that human dialogue can exist outside boundaries of verbal communication. If it were limited to only verbal communication, it would not penetrate deep into the sacred areas of the human experience. Genuine dialogue moves deep into a place where those involved can openly share their feelings and thoughts. Buber (1947/2002) referred to the sharing of feelings and thoughts as communion. He wrote, "But I can really show what I have in mind only by events which open into a genuine change communication to communion, that is an embodiment of the word of dialogue" (p. 6). As a scholar, a translator, and an interpreter of the Torah, Buber may have attributed a deeper meaning to communion. Communion in the context that Buber could have understood it comes from the word *kninōnia*, which means to have in common and to share in anything (i.e., share in good things and in suffering; Vine et al., 1980/1985). This type of sharing requires more than cursory involvement; people must fully turn to each other, fully engage, and thereby perceive the other.

Buber (1947/2002) listed several ways a person perceives others. First, an observer is one who studies the other and sees only the traits of the other—things like hair color, height, dress, and maybe even personal hygiene, etc. This person makes no demands or connections to the other. He or she is only concerned with gathering the surface information. Second, an onlooker sees the other but does not even make note of the other's traits. The observer and the onlooker do not seek to fully engage with the other; their wish is to glean surface information without input from the other. And third, one perceives the other by becoming aware of the other. Becoming aware of the other entails being completely engaged with the other in ways that the other is not an object to be studied but a being to be experienced. Buber's third way of perception is what is desired for genuine dialogue to take place.

Buber (1947/2002) provided three different kinds of dialogue. First, genuine dialogue is a verbal or nonverbal interaction where each participant turns to the other with the intention of creating a living mutual relationship. Second, technical dialogue is used to acquire objective understanding. And third, monologue disguised as dialogue is the interaction that appears to be dialogue but the inner reactions and thoughts brought on by turning are not addressed by either participant. Kramer (2003) wrote,

> Dialogue becomes genuine when each of the participants is fully present to the other or others, openly attentive to all voices, and willing to be nonjudgmental. Dialogue becomes technical when the need to understand something, or gain information, is the focal point of the exchange. Dialogue becomes in fact monologue when one participant is only interested in imposing his or her point of view to the exclusion of all other views. (p. 33)

Genuine dialogue is the preferred form of dialogue when attempting to connect with the other in a prolonged and profound way. The type of interactions that Buber spoke of in genuine dialogue mirrors the interactions sought by people of faith between themselves and God. It is obvious that Buber's faith system was intricately woven through his ideas concerning dialogue. He used his view to show the genuine relationship between God and man—one of intimacy, trust, transparency, and security—as shown in the very Hebrew scriptures he interpreted. The God of the Torah is continuously calling to man to be in genuine relationship with Him, as evident by his call in Isaiah for us, as a people, to come and reason with him. Buber (1970) called the God of the Torah the "eternal Thou."

Kramer (2003) believes that the central theme of Buber's work was focused on the relationship between beings. Kramer wrote, concerning Buber, "The central tenet of his life's work was that the I-Thou relationships between persons intimately reflects the I-Thou relationship humans have with God. Genuine relationship with any thou shows glimpses of the 'eternal Thou'" (p. 24).

Buber (1970) believed that the space created between I and Thou is where the real life-changing, powerfully pregnant, meaning-making experience takes place. This place is referred to as the "between." The "between" produces the conditions conducive for chrysalis metamorphism. The between is also the place where we can catch a glimpse of the "eternal Thou." Kramer (2003) stated, "Reading through I and Thou, it thus becomes clear that Buber's dialogical stand is inseparable from his view that God not only can be glimpsed in genuine dialogue, but also reaches out to humans by penetrating the realm of the between" (p. 25).

In order for I and Thou to have genuine dialogue, they must first meet, which is turning to the other completely, as we've previously discussed. Meeting is turning to the Thou completely in the present moment and "completely" as person to whole person (Kramer, 2003). Complete turning requires a great deal of trust and a willingness to be vulnerable to the other. Kramer claimed that dialogic participants, in order to achieve dialogical wholeness, must be willing to surrender and act. People must wave the "white flag" and not fight against the openness this process requires and, then, be willing to act on what surfaces.

Trust is a very important aspect of meeting. When there is no trust, there is no connection. A person's affective filter blocks all attempts at communication. The affective filter is the person's attempt to defend and protect himself or herself when he or she is experiencing anxiety and discomfort. The higher the person's level of trust, the lower the person's level of the affective filter will be. "Trusting a person means, at least for Buber, that whatever this person may do, say, or become, I am willing to accept him or her not as an object of my experience but as a human being" (Kramer, 2003, p. 46).

When there is no trust, the people will "mis-meet." Kramer (2003) pointed out that "genuine meeting, Buber discovered, requires unconditional trust, a willingness to be vulnerable to the other" (p. 46). Kramer continued by listing several reasons people will mis-meet. The first reason for mis-meeting is one person dismissing the other, where one is not counting what the other communicates as valid. Secondly, a person might misrecognize the other by not being able or willing to see the other as he or she is. Lastly, there could be miscommunication with the other, where the individuals are not able to generate meaning because incorrect meaning is applied to what is communicated.

The most important experience a human being can have is found in turning toward the other. Buber (1947/2002) posited that a person's ability to turn toward the other is connected to his or her connection to God, the "Supreme Other." He also pointed out that the eternal Thou actually meets those in dialogue in the space created between them when they fully turn toward each other.

> In turning one drops facades or the need to seem to be different than one really is. Swinging outward, one turns toward the other person and, in the process, toward "the between," through which the presence of the "eternal Thou" can be glimpsed. When turning is mutual, a "memorable common fruitfulness" is brought into existence. Each person stimulates and is stimulated by a meaningful newness that bonds the two." (Kramer, 2003, p. 160)

Most people, however, fail to notice the sacredness of their interactions. Kramer (2003) also wrote,

> In I and Thou, "spirit" (*Geist*) is named as an essential element of person-with-person meetings . . . . Buber suggests that the "component" of interpersonal relationship that often remains hidden, or goes unnoticed,

The Transcultural Leader, Leading the Way to PCA

is "spirit." Spirit, called in the King James Bible "the breath of life," is closely related to spoken language, address and response. It is the very breath required for language to work. (p. 59)

The act of becoming fully aware of the other is the optimal way to connect with the other because the other is then allowed to become what it is through your interaction. Figures 6 and 7 illustrate Buber's turning and connecting process.

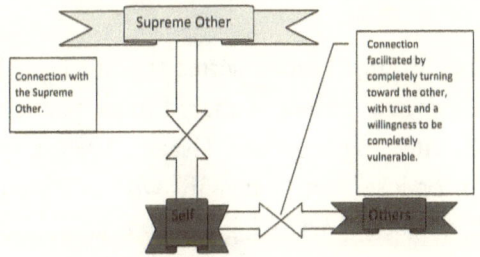

Figure 6. Connection to Supreme Other facilitates connection to self and others

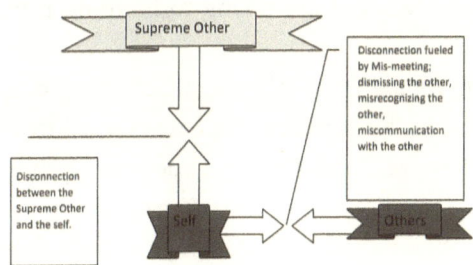

Figure 7. Disconnection from the Supreme Other facilitates disconnection from self and others.

dialogue.

Buberian dialogic principles focus mainly on two individuals being fully present with each other. He correlated the ability to connect with others to the ability to reach outside of oneself to a Supreme Other. This gives dialogue a sense of sacredness and provides the transcendence needed to reach above the manmade barriers to dialogue. Bohm (1996) gave dialogue an earthly feel. He described what happens when people "turn" toward each other. The next section provides a down-to-earth description of the interactions inside oneself and between others that provides the trans-cultural leader with the nuts and bolts needed to create a culture of dialogue.

David Bohm. Bohm (1996) asserted that dialogue is not a debate. "Dialogue is about a shared inquiry, a way of thinking and reflecting together" (Isaacs, 1999, p. 9) There is no "win or lose" but "win-win" when dialogue takes place. Bohm wrote, "In a dialogue, however, nobody is trying to win. Everybody wins if anybody wins" (p. 7). This captures the overall objective of dialogue, where we are not trying to beat each other into submission with our lofty words and ideas but are trying to build each other up with them.

Every individual, culture, and society has its own views, concerns, understandings, and ways of addressing each other. However, the human experience produces commonalities from which humans can draw. "In a dialogue each person does not attempt to make common certain ideas or items of information that are already known to him. Rather, it may be said that the two people are making something in common" (Bohm, 1996, p. 3).

Many people equate dialogue with negotiating, which is a give-and-take process. In negotiations, each side usually gives up something and there is no joining of ideas or shared meaning because each side is trying to win. Isaacs (1999) stated,

> The aim of negotiation is to reach agreement among parties who differ. The intention of dialogue is to reach new understanding and in doing so, to form a totally new basis from which to think and act. In dialogue, one not only solves problems, one dissolves them. (p. 19)

It appears that negotiating automatically puts people on the defensive. Genuine dialogue, however, does not put people on the defensive.

One of the goals of dialogue is to change the collective thought process, which is very culturally orientated. A person learns how to think through his or her interactions with the outside world. When a group of people share similar obstacles and successfully overcome them, the group develops a collective way of describing and interacting with the outside world. Bohm (1996) wrote that "the individual thought is mostly the result of collective thought and of interaction with other people" (p. 15). Bohm believed that thought was the problem. He believed people's thought processes lead to assumptions and opinions. Problems arise when people feel as though they have to defend their assumptions and opinions. A person's succumbing to the need to defending leads to the end of a dialogic process. The participants of a dialogue must understand that dialogue is an attempt to allow meaning to flow, not to suppress differing views.

Bohm (1996) applied the terms *coherence* and *incoherence* to the thought process, which, to him, explained the process of applying the knowledge one has at a certain point to a particular issue. Incoherence of thought occurs when a person applies his or her limited level of thought to the situation at hand. A male teacher who has taught sixth grade for 20 years may have a goal to improve the standardized testing scores of his students by 10%. He institutes his 20-year-old tested-and-tried test improvement strategy of intensely focused lectures, but the students' scores drop drastically. The teacher's intentions were to improve test scores by lecturing more, but the results were opposite. This would be an example of incoherence.

According to Bohm, incoherence is to be expected, and it is actually the road to coherence. The journey to coherence is acknowledgement of the incoherence followed by a willingness to add to, completely change, or simply acknowledge a different view. Problems occur when an individual is not willing to change his or her knowledge base and actually defends it. So, the teacher mentioned above, even though his students' scores dropped, insists that his way works and he "tries harder." His thoughts that because it worked before it had to work again resulted in an attempt to recreate it which became his "idol." According to Isaacs (1999), something becomes an idol when a person's positive outcome in the past with a particular situation or event becomes the person's reference point on which all else is based. The thought is not new or original;

rather, it is based on some bygone experience. Dialogue is about seeking new and fresh meaning.

Coherence, on the other hand, occurs when the teacher understands that direct instruction in the form of lectures works to a limited degree with sixth graders. However, he knows that learning increases when as many of the students' learning modalities as possible are utilized, and he changes his strategy as needed. In order for the teacher to reach his state of coherence, he has to experience incoherence, acknowledge it, and be willing to change.

Dialogue is about shared meaning, not about total agreement. Agreement may never come, but meaning will and can increase. Understanding where the other "is coming from," even if there is no agreement, can still produce cooperative action. Yankelovich (1999) put less emphasis on harmony and more on understanding when defining dialogue. He wrote, "The outcome of dialogue is not always harmony. In fact, as a consequence of dialogue you may come to understand why you disagree so vehemently with someone else; there will be better understanding, but not necessarily more harmony" (p. 14).

Truth is not the ultimate goal of dialogue because one person may believe that he or she knows the "truth" and the other does not, which could stunt the dialogic process. "Therefore, you have to watch out for the notion of truth. Dialogue may not be concerned directly with truth—it may arrive at truth, but it is concerned with meaning" (Bohm, 1996, p. 43).

This concept seemed very difficult for me to accept because my faith system teaches that there is an "ultimate" truth that we all run towards. In reading Bohm, I had to suspend my initial reaction in order to "dialogue" with the text, which is different from dialoguing with a person. Bernstein (1983) pointed out that there is a difference because text is fixed. However, upon intentional interaction with the text, it opens like the chrysalis into a beautiful butterfly. My interaction with Bohm's text was a very uncomfortable process. However, after reminding myself that there is no need to agree but only the need to share meaning, my effective filter lowered, and I concluded that this "truth" Bohm spoke of is not the "truth" of which my faith system speaks. I had to determine in my heart to read without judgment because judgment would have ended my critical interaction with the text. Bohm (1996) believed that blocks to dialogue include an unwillingness to listen without judgment and an unwillingness to disengage assumptions. He believed that religious people would have the hardest time with the dialogic process.

He wrote,

> Religious people would be the hardest to get together. The assumption of the different religions are so firmly embedded that I don't know of any case of two religions, or even subgroups of any given religion, where they ever got together once they had split. The Christian church, for instance, has been talking about trying to get together for ages and it stays about the same all the time. They talk and they appear to get a little closer, and then it never happens. They talk about unity and oneness and love, and all that, but

> the other assumptions are more powerful; they are programmed into us. Some religious people are trying to get together; they are really sincere—they are as serious as they can be—but it seems that they cannot do it. (p. 14)

However, the words of an early church father show the contrary. Saint Augustine of Hippo's assertion for the church to be unified in the essentials and to have liberty in the nonessentials allows the Christian Church to come together and to have the essentials as the common ground on which to stand. The difficulty comes when religious groups of differing faith systems attempt to "come together." Coming together for purposeful action is possible as long as the adherents to their respective faith systems understand that they are not seeking total agreement but shared meaning. Bohm (1996) asserted, "There is no conflict in the fact that the individual does not agree. It's not all that important whether you agree or not. There is no pressure to agree or disagree" (p. 37). An understanding that there is no need in the dialogic process to do away with one's "essential views" is the key to a person of faith's total engagement. It could possibly add to the process. Buber (1947/2002) wrote in *Between Man and Man*,

> When it comes to the question of "essential views" conversations must not be broken off, each person must turn completely to the other so that they both experience the uncomfortable season together. He continues

Dr. Jonathan E. Smith

> to assert that, "neither needs to give up his point of view." (p. 7)

People have to experience discomfort in order to add to the collective mind. If coming together could occur in the religious world, which is admittedly more difficult, it would work in the secular world as well. I believe that if a person of faith is well grounded in his or her belief system, then that person will not be afraid to suspend judgment and engage in the dialogic process. Once the urge to defend prevails, dialogue dies.

Holding on to and defending assumptions is the fuel that runs the "incoherence train." Bohm (1996) provided the reader with several other blocks to dialogue, one of which is the participant's inability to understand that a person's past affects his or her actions. The dialogic process could trigger certain reactions from the participants because the process places the individual in a position that questions what he or she has learned in the past. The realization that what the participant has learned may be wrong or in need of adjusting triggers a stance of defense, which could manifest in several ways. Bohm's blocks could be a manifestation of the defensive stance. A person may assert himself or herself, hold back, or attempt to speed up the dialogic process in an attempt to move past the uncomfortable points in the process.

The blocks mentioned above can and will disrupt the dialogic process. Because assumptions are the product of past thoughts, most people have them. The issue is when we feel compelled to defend our assumptions. We, as human beings, may have issues we consider taboo and react strongly when that belief is threatened. Bohm (1996) posited, "In the sense that there are all sorts of things which are held to be non-negotiable and un-touchable, and people don't even want to talk about them. That is part of our trouble" (p. 8). He referred to this as thoughts of necessity, thoughts that will not be turned aside. Perhaps this is true to a point, but I believe that people have certain thoughts or beliefs that they are not willing to "turn aside." As previously mentioned, Buber (1947/2002) believed that such thoughts, "essential views," should be a part of the dialogue and could possibly add to the dialogic process. This can be an emotional process and has the potential of being a deal breaker if not navigated with care. Bohm's navigational tool is suspending.

Dialogical participants must learn how to suspend their reactions. The purpose of suspension is to allow the participant to look inside and analyze his or her thoughts, without ascribing positive or negative descriptions to the assumption. Bohm (1996) wrote, "To suspend those assumptions, so that you neither carry them out nor suppress them. You don't believe them, nor do you disbelieve them; you don't judge them as good or bad" (p. 23). Suspension is a very important aspect of dialogue. If an individual is able to belay his or her initial reactions long enough to prevent his or her affective filter from rising, then that individual can then hear the other and consider his or her point of view.

Dialogue's aim is to share meaning and to develop a "collective consciousness." The sense of one body and one mind is accomplished through suspending, where, according to Bohm (1996), everyone listens to each others' opinions even if they agree or not. "The individual might hold a separate opinion, but that opinion would then be absorbed into the group" (Bohm, 1996, p. 31). The idea is that in a culture of dialogue all the divergent views and opinions converge, not losing their uniqueness but adding their uniqueness to the collective. The collective is not concerned with finding the "obvious" answer but only with the meaning that is shared. Bohm wrote,

> The object of dialogue is not to analyze things, or to win an argument, or to exchange opinions. Rather, it is to suspend your opinions and to look at the opinions—to listen to everybody's opinions, to suspend them, and to see what all that means. If we can see what all of our opinions mean, then we are sharing a common content, even if we don't agree entirely. (p. 30)

Bohm (1996) believed that if people with assumptions are not willing to be challenged, the result of that resistance dampens the dialogic process. He referred to this as thoughts of necessity. According to Bohm (1996), once a person believes something is a necessity, problems in dialogue occur. Buber also referred to opinions and views that people may consider to be taboo as essential views. Buber, however, encouraged the participants in the dialogic process to be present with the tension that may arise because it will add to the process. It is important for those involved in the dialogic process to realize they are not required to agree with the other; they are required to seek to understand the other. Suspension is the key

The Transcultural Leader, Leading the Way to PCA

to dialogue. One must be able to suspend his or her reactions long enough to hear the other. Only then can the participants share meaning.

Suspension is the key to dialogue. One must be able to suspend his or her reactions long enough to hear the other. Only then can the participants share meaning. Figure 7 shows how Bohm sees the connection process between individuals.

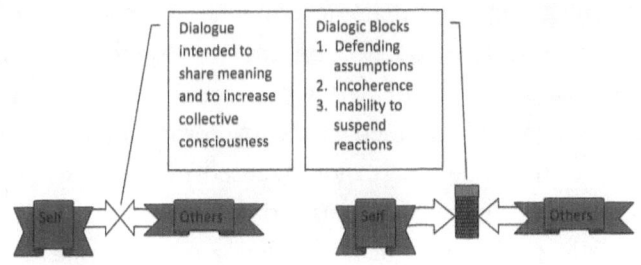

Figure 8. Summing up Bohmian dialogue

Types of dialogue. The Buberian and Bohmian approaches to dialogue may contain a more overarching umbrella in application. Buber focused on the interaction between two beings, and Bohm geared his approach toward larger groups of people. Each is intended to flow indefinitely. These two approaches are like a vast river in which meaning flows, but there comes a time when the power of the river must be harnessed and applied to a specific topic or situation. Buber used the term *technical dialogue* when the primary focus is on gaining information (Kramer, 2003). Bohm (1996) identified dialogue that has a purpose and a goal in mind as "limited dialogue."

He added that it is best to be open in dialogue, but, "if people are not ready to be completely open in their communication, they should do what they can" (p. 49). It is obvious that Bohm did not prefer this type of interaction but reluctantly saw the need for its application.

Trans-cultural leaders must be able to create a culture of dialogue in their organizations, a culture that allows meaning to flow freely and continuously. But there comes a time when decisions must be made. In those times, one must focus the dialogic flow on the issue at hand. Hargrove (2003) touched on the idea of focusing on the issue at hand when he wrote about a collaborative conversation. He alluded to a conversation that has the spirit of dialogue but is more focused in its application. Senge (1990) wrote that a team that has regular dialogue can effectively move between dialogue and discussion. He posited that discussion is a necessary counterpart to dialogue. In discussion, ideas are brought forward, some of which make it and others which fall on the cutting room floor. This happens after a prolonged dialogic encounter, where trust has been established. There can be a continuous turning from dialogue to discussion that is not totally destructive, but it may require a facilitator. Bohm (1996) realized the usefulness of a facilitator in dialogue when he wrote, "It is useful to have a facilitator to 'jump start' the dialogic process" (p. 17).

"In a genuine dialogue or conversation, what is to be understood guides the movement of the dialogue" (Bernstein, 1983, p. 162). When there is a need to understand how to solve a particular problem, dialogue moves from that which is open to that which is focused.

Yankelovich (1999) wrote about the need to move from dialogue to decision-making. He posited that dialogue and decision-making should never happen at the same time.

> Even when the sole purpose of a dialogue is to reach a decision, the dialogue part of the process should precede the decision-making part . . . for truly difficult decisions, the act of seeking mutual understanding through dialogue should come before all of the practical constraints and clash of interests involved in practical decision making are brought to bear. (Yankelovich, 1999, p. 57)

In any organization, decisions need to be made, and the process could be much easier if done in a culture of dialogue. "The primary difference between dialogue and skillful discussion is intention" (Bell, 1996, p. 20).

Dialogue brings different cultures (i.e., races, genders, professions, disciplines, etc.) toward cultural cohorting. This is done first in genuine dialogue because that is the place where assumptions are addressed and connections are made, as mentioned above. Banathy and Jenlink (2005) wrote, "Dialogue offers the possibility of creating new cultures across differences, using differences as the very energy that fires social and cultural creativity" (p. 7). This new culture will have the ability to fluidly move from genuine dialogue to a place where decisions can be made. Banathy and Jenlink suggested that "dialogue may be transformative or generative in nature, as well as strategic" (p. 5). Transformative or generative dialogue is the type of dialogue proposed by both Buber (1947/2002) and Bohm (1996), which was discussed in detail above. Strategic dialogue is dialogue that is intended to produce a solution. Some may call strategic dialogue a skillful discussion, which could be loosely likened to Buber's technical dialogue. For a group to move easily from generative to strategic dialogue, the group must "live" in a culture of dialogue. The trans-cultural leader must encourage and foster the formation of the culture of dialogue. Hicks (2008) wrote, "Whether people within an organization practice dialogue are largely determined by culture—company-wide, or within a department or division. The good news is that leadership can shape culture to encourage wider and deeper dialogue" (p. 17).

There are two forms of dialogue. Generative dialogue flows like a river teeming with understanding and meaning, with no determined direction or agenda but only to share meaning. Strategic dialogue can be likened to a structure not as restrictive as a dam but is able to divert the flow to cultivate solutions to the problems at hand, which could lead to purposeful cooperative action. Once a solution is found, the flow continues on as it was before, possibly with additional information to add to the collective consciousness.

The Transcultural Leader, Leading the Way to PCA

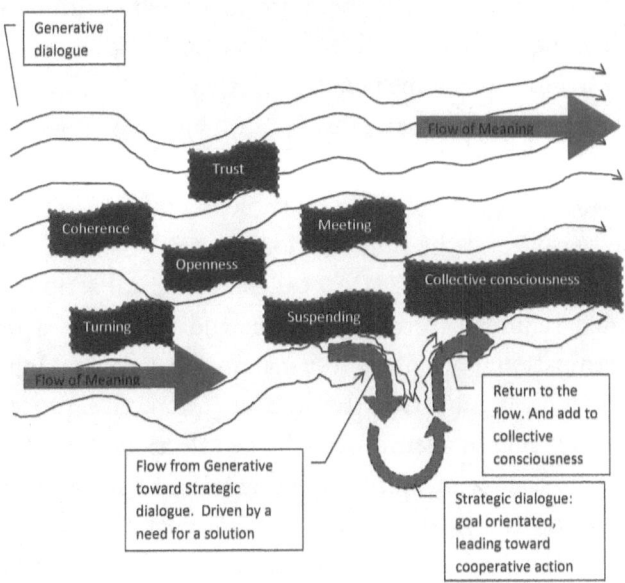

Figure 9. Flow from generative dialogue to strategic dialogue and back again

Figure 9 shows the generative dialogic process, where the concepts offered by Bohm and Buber lead to a collective consciousness that moves the river along. When there is a need for a solution, the flow can be diverted and applied to strategic dialogue, which could lead to cooperative action. Once the group arrives at a solution, they return to the flow, possibly with more information to add to the collective consciousness.

Application of dialogue. Dialogue is an age-old concept in which we all should aspire to engage, in some form or another. It seems to be the nature of people to want some approved protocol instructing them how to do something. The same holds true for those seeking to facilitate dialogue. There are many who admit that "dialogue does not follow any recipe" (Brown, 2005, p. 57). However, some people still attempt to ascribe some type of process to dialogue.

Oswick, Anthony, Keenoy, Mangham, and Grant (2000) acknowledged that dialogue is a process in which the person and the organization connect. Oswick et al. employed an approach they called "dialogical scripting," which requires a group to select and reflect on a real organizational event as the catalyst for developing a fictionalized narrative through an interactive process. The first step in their process is the selection of an event or issue that is meaningful and significant for all those involved. The next step is to reconstruct the event by having the participants record the information. The group would then reconstitute reality by thinking of alternative ways of seeing the event. Oswick et al. called this a move toward "dialogic fiction." They believe this would allow the participants to move toward deeper underlying issues. Finally, the group would reflect on the issues and the process in order to have deeper and collective insight. Oswick et al. posited that dialogical scripting shares similarities with appreciative inquiry because of the sharing of positive stories of the past and a basis of mutual generation of direction for the future.

The steps provided by Oswick et al. (2000) are very detailed, and the practitioner could become so bogged down trying to stick to the script that the process is lost in the details. It may be more advantageous for a trans-cultural leader to concentrate on understanding the characteristics of dialogue and creating an environment conducive for generative and strategic dialogue.

Brown (2005) pointed out that dialogue has certain characteristics. One is that people in the dialogic process see others as different because, according to Brown, we do not engage until we see others as being different from ourselves. If we are the same, we are not curious. The state of being curious leads us to the second characteristic of asking questions of inquiry in order to find out something we do not know. We then are led to the third characteristic of acknowledging the differences we may discover, which leads us to the undiscovered country of the unknown. Through this undiscovered country, we find common ground. Kersten (2000) wrote,

> Dialogue of any sort assumes at its minimum that participants have the capacity to understand and acknowledge their own worldview and express it competently. It also assumes that they are able to grasp the worldview of the other and, through discourse, develop some kind of language and common ground. (p. 238)

Kersten added that dialogue asks for a critical and reflective understanding of the participant's own world, empathy for others, and the ability to share in the building of a joint world.

In order to create an environment conducive to dialogue, one must be encouraged to understand who he or she is, and why he or she believes what he or she believes. One must also have a level of empathy for fellow humans and be willing to create something new. Therefore, some additional characteristics of dialogue are self-awareness on behalf of the participants, empathy for others, and creativity. Bokeno (2007) added that dialogue is dynamic, in that it flows and changes. "Dialogue requires open, honest, mutual interaction; not clearer messages but authentic collaboration, not more communication, but different communication, trust, genuine self-reflection, exposure of clear and tacit ways of thinking, and willingness to grow through risk" (Bokeno, 2007, p. 9).

Isaacs (1999) asked, "How can we learn, as individuals, to take actions that might be conductive to evoking dialogue?" (p. 29). This question shows the importance of creating an environment that encourages the development of a culture of dialogue. In order for a tans-cultural leader to bring the many to one in purpose, vision, and action, that leader must be able to create a safe place for all those involved. A trans-cultural leader must understand, as Yankelovich (1999) pointed out, that dialogue occurs in environments that promote equality, that are truly empathizing, and that promote assumption revelation and respectful consideration. There can be no hierarchy in the dialogic process because that causes individuals not to share their deepest concerns, for fear of reprisals from superiors. When points of view surface and vulnerabilities arise, empathy goes a long way in the connection process. It is of supreme importance for a person to demonstrate to the other person that he or she understands or wants to understand the position of the other. Also, all assumptions must be revealed and given respectful consideration. The moment a person feels that his or her views are not being considered and that person feels unheard, connection is impossible.

Hicks (2008) presented a list of six ways to engage in dialogue. Most of his ways match those listed above. Hicks's addition to the previous list, which calls for being prepared, shows the importance of living in dialogue, always being ready to connect with the other, and always prepared to share in the flow of meaning. I find it interesting that Hicks, like Brown (2005), mentioned curiosity. One must be eternally curious in order to learn and grow. There is always that yearning within humans to connect with others and learn together, but most lack the tools to fulfill that need. Ballantyne (2004) wrote that dialogue is an interactive process of learning together. He added that the relationship generated by such interactions fosters trust, which allows growing and evolving together. The transcultural leader must be able to create an environment that encourages interaction, builds trust, and provides room for growth and change.

The trans-cultural leader must live in dialogue and must be able to create a dialogic environment. This type of leader, as Brown (2005) stated, must be curious and willing to inquire, and learn and go to the unknown. He or she must have earned the trust of his or her followers and be willing to be vulnerable. The trans-cultural leader must not seek to create hundreds of versions of himself or herself but be able to create strength out of diversity. "Dialogue does not eliminate differences, rather through dialogue; participants create a consciousness of differences that can sustain differences within a larger social compact of toleration and respect" (Banathy & Jenlink, 2005,

p. 11). There must be a respect and understanding of differences.

> Diversity in the workplace includes all differences that define each of us as unique individuals. Differences such as culture, ethnicity, race, gender, nationality, age, religion, disability, sexual orientation, education, experiences, opinions and beliefs are just some of the distinctions we each bring to the workplace. (Kersten, 2000, p. 242)

As mentioned above, the trans-cultural leader must be able to lead above the barriers put in place by these differences. Unfortunately, as pointed out by Ballantyne (2004), "Organizations can unintentionally create systemic constraints which obstruct dialogue and inhibit people from learning together . . . each boundary is the end of a zone of likeness and the beginning of a zone of difference" (p. 118). Therefore, a trans-cultural leader must have a firm grasp of the concepts of dialogue and must be able to lead his or her group in and out of generative and strategic dialogue.

The trans-cultural leader creates an environment that encourages true meeting between individuals and groups and maintains a safe place that allows assumptions to come to the light in order to be examined and, perhaps, challenged. Ballantyne (2004) argued that dialogue offers a new pathway to business knowledge when he wrote, "Dialogical interactions help trust develop between participants, and this facilitates learning and the generation of knowledge" (p. 114).

Varney (1996) suggested dialogue leads to the emergence of the "mind of the organization" (p. 32). Participants develop a transcendence that frees them from deep cultural conditioning. Dialogue is the key to transcendence. The trans-cultural leader's greatest job is to reproduce others who are able to transcend cultural barriers and move toward cooperative action.

IV

Trans-cultural Leadership Undergirded Culture, Life Journey, and Dialogue

Trans-cultural leaders must have a grasp of the concepts discussed above in order to lead people towards purposeful cooperative action. Now we will discuss those concepts as they have been applied by trans-cultural leaders from different fields.

Understanding of culture applied. Research (Smith, 2010) shows that a Trans-cultural leader leads by having an understanding of culture as it relates to organizational and social settings. Roni is the CEO and president of a large organ and tissue procurement agency, which procures organs and tissue for transplantation to patients who need this life-saving service. Roni's comments began with the initial statements indicating that he is a leader who is culturally aware, culturally competent, and culturally open. He demonstrated that he has an understanding of culture as it relates to his organization by stating that culture is extremely important in the organization. He commented, "What we do is very complex and very multifaceted; it involves doctors, scientists, engineers, and donor families." When asked about his knowledge of culture, he discussed the culture of the organization and included the people outside the organization that he serves. Roni showed that he is aware of the cultures in the organization and considers the differences that exist among them.

Before working in his current position, Roni ran a very successful diagnostic imaging business. When he first began employment at his present company, he realized that it would be a "great mission for him to undertake." He noticed that it was a very small organization that had the potential to do great things. Roni believes that his understanding of culture helps him in his present position because he came from a very "capitalistic, hard-core, business-oriented company" to a company that deals with the humanitarian acts of donating tissue. That, in itself, according to Roni, requires good cultural knowledge. Roni's conversations about culture were focused on organizational culture; he generated cultural knowledge by being an astute observer of the cultures he encounters in both secular and business environments.

Joe, an administrator of a 165-bed psychiatric residential treatment center, showed his understanding of culture by stating that he believes the culture of an institution holds a standard by which people often pattern their behaviors and that the culture can be changed. Joe was very open concerning his presentation of his transcultural leadership experiences. His initial statement was about culture: "I see culture as something that starts at the top, and everybody from the top to the bottom should see what the culture is and try to convince others to be a part of it." This statement shows his level of cultural awareness and competence. Joe recalled that when he first started working at his present facility, the culture was not necessarily what he envisioned, so he had to embark on a journey to change the culture. His understanding of culture helped him because he knew that culture is different wherever you live, and he had the good fortune of moving around the country and living in many different places. Joe provided an example.

> The culture here in Virginia is very different than the culture in Miami. People's culture has a lot to do with the type environment they were bought up in; for example, I was bought up in a very rural area and then moved to San Francisco, which is very busy and fast, so I had to learn to adapt.

Joe's having to adapt to several different cultures helped him to be sensitive to cultures around him. He stated, "My understanding of culture helped me in the sense of knowing, if the culture is dysfunctional, then the relationships within the culture will be dysfunctional." Based on the pervious quote, it appears that Joe devotes considerable time thinking about culture as it applies to his organization. His understanding of culture and his organization allowed him to understand the importance of being relational, which can be seen in his report that when he first arrived at the organization he "started to

Dr. Jonathan E. Smith

develop relationships with others" in order to feel the pulse of the organization. Joe's ideas about leading transculturally called for him to look at what was around him and to realize that the organization does not exist in a bubble or a vacuum; he was aware that everyone at his facility are very talented, are from different environments, and have different ways of doing things.

Alma is the executive director of a California-based organization that is comprised of lawyers and various artists. When describing what her company does, one of her earliest statements referred to the cultural context of their work. Alma demonstrated her understanding of culture by stating that she believes that hard work in the service organization helps bridge the gaps between cultures: "We seek to help people bridge the assumptions that come from different cultural contexts," she stated. She explained that misunderstandings happen around communication, and much of that is based on cultural assumptions. This leader's ability to be culturally competent was alluded to when she stated, "I think that being respectful of everyone's cultural backgrounds, what their issues are, and what their interests are is very important."

Alma's background was actually in the mediation field, and her first job in the organization was that of mediator. She admitted that she is quite tuned in to being mindful of others and encouraging people to work well together. She said she understands she cannot do all things by herself, and she has to encourage others to do their part.

At the time of the interview, Keith owned several businesses, including a cardiology practice, a nonprofit foundation, and a jazz club, and he was the principal of a PLLC. Keith approached the interviews with confident assurance. He was not arrogant, even though he had achieved a great deal of his goals at a relatively young age. Our conversations provided good insight into his experiences as a leader of several organizations comprised of various organizational and ethnic cultures. His initial statement showed me that he is culturally aware when he defined culture as "a mindset that often times is based on how you grew up and your surroundings and your upbringing." The previous statement demonstrates that this leader has a broad view of culture and an understanding that there are external influences to the development of culture. Keith showed that he able to expand perspective, explore options, and create alternatives by not limiting himself to one aspect of his life.

Life's Journey. A trans-cultural leader's life experiences helps in their leading others today. As mentioned earlier, trans-cultural leadership can be seen as a quest or a journey in that every life obstacle and accomplishment contributes to the development of the leader.

Keith stated that dedication, tenacity, and a purpose helped him to get to the position that he currently holds. He noted that he believes leaders must always sacrifice because people are more willing to follow leaders who will make sacrifices for them. Keith values his personal life and draws on that as he leads trans-culturally. He mentioned his family several times during the interviews. He first mentioned his family when he was deciding where he wanted to attend medical school, which was significant to him because his first daughter had just been born and he was also responsible for caring for his mother. Keith said, "When I chose to go to medical school, I had to consider my mother because my father was already deceased and my mother depended on me and my siblings . . . . I also had to consider my wife because she just had my first child." He stated that the decision of where to attend medical school may have felt like it was selfish, but he believes that trans-cultural leaders have to make decisions that may seem selfish at first but helps everyone else in the long run, which showed his concern for the common good. He said that the decision he made was another thing that allowed him to be in the position that he now holds and to help people who he is helping now. Keith said, "You must sacrifice and show that you are really concerned about the well-being of those who follow you." His life experience at making difficult decisions based on his family's needs contributed to his actions as a trans-cultural leader today.

Joe started working in his field 15 years ago and worked his way up from being a mental health counselor to an administrator. He attributes his success to his understanding of people and the different roles that they play in residential settings. Before Joe came to the facility in which he was employed at the time of the interview, he was the CEO of a similar company at three different facilities. He mentioned that the culture at the previous company in which he worked was not compatible with his vision, so he chose to move to his current organization.

Joe explained that he sees his mission as providing the most therapeutic environment possible for his residents. In order for him to do that, he had to rely on his senior management team, which is comprised of a director of clinical services, a medical director, admissions, human resources, education, dietary, custodial, and three program managers. He mentioned that he believes his task is to help all these different professionals to "be on the same page" so that they can create the best therapeutic environment for the residents. He stated that as an administrator it is "important to understand what everyone brings to the table and it is vital to create opportunities for growth, which could make any organization stronger."

Joe reported that he realized he wanted to be a leader very early in life. He tied his aspirations for leadership to his athletic ventures in high school and college. He said he likes to be challenged, and he likes to challenge others to be at their best. He also attributed his upbringing and the traditions he learned in his life for shaping who he is today as a leader. Joe shared that he grew up on a ranch, and he had to work with the cows twice a day. It was not just a job, it was a lifestyle, and he had no option whether or not he would do it. He admitted that his father taught him the meaning of hard work. However, he said that his father was more of a dictator in his leadership style. When asked why he was not a dictator-style leader, he commented that he had learned that "leading by intimidation does not work. Motivation works well for me."

Roni attributed his leadership abilities to his early life experiences. His parents were educators who taught him the value of education and the value of respecting differences. His family traveled often when he was a child, as evidenced by the fact that he was born in Ethiopia and lived in India and America. Roni's life experiences seemed to have helped him to "interact with people that have many differences." Living in many parts of the world and being exposed to many different groups of people easily translated to his ability to work with different organizational cultures. To Roni, leading trans-culturally is a "natural" extension of who he is.

Alma did not see herself as a leader when she was younger. She shared with me that she grew up in North Carolina was an only child. She added, "My family was split because my mother worked in another town and had to commute often. So, I was mostly raised by grandparents." I assumed that being an only child and spending so much time with her grandparents she would have been bored, but Alma stated, "I was not very bored as a child living with my grandfather and grandmother because my grandfather would take me around with him; my grandmother gave me music lessons. They kept me very busy, actually." Alma attributed her work ethic to spending so much time with her grandparents. She shared that her grandfather was a hard-working man, and, when he came home, he expected everyone to be doing something. Alma also mentioned that her grandmother was a devoted Jehovah's Witness, and she took Alma on several evangelistic outings. Alma said she believes the trips she took with her grandmother to evangelize strengthened her ability to speak to strangers and make them feel at ease with her.

Each of these trans-cultural leaders utilized their life's journeys' experiences to deepen their abilities to lead others. Their quest, riddled with successes and failures, dreams fulfilled and differed all add to the fulfillment their life's call to lead. The next section illustrates the trans-cultural leaders' understanding and facilitation of dialogue.

Dialogue utilized. Rony commented that he believes his best quality is his ability to build consensus with others. He stated, "I believe in teamwork, and when you come to my organization, you will see that teamwork plays a major part. I have surrounded myself with some of the smartest people in the industry." Dialogue plays a major role in Rony's organization. He asserted that he has an open-door policy and welcomes challenges from others. He said he believes that the key is that people have learned to trust him and people understand that regardless of what they say about a certain situation; they will not be in the doghouse for speaking their minds. He admitted that his dialogues become very spirited, but this kind of interaction fosters the development of trust and connection. He commented about an incident during a retreat where one of his senior leaders told him that it was good to have an atmosphere where he could speak openly and not fear repercussions. Rony commented that the observation made by his senior leader was stunning to him because he always thought that openness and trust were the foundation of good leadership and was sadden when he realized that it was not the norm.

Dr. Jonathan E. Smith

I asked Rony how he managed to balance leading his organization from a trans-cultural perspective and the need for attention to the bottom line. He answered the question by asserting that a leader cannot choose between dialogue and the bottom line. He stated he believes that the time spent on creating an environment conducive for dialogue actually helps with the bottom line. He said, "Basically, we tie everything into the dialogue in the organization, because we have quick and intelligent managers and vice-presidents who are capable of making appropriate decisions." The appropriate decisions come from meeting every day for 45 minutes to discuss issues, and those meetings generate the familiarity needed to make hard decisions quickly and efficiently." Rony indicated that the "bottom line and dialogue are not mutually exclusive."

Keith indicated that he allows room for dialogue in all of his businesses. He said, "I find that I am more open to discussion if the other person is as invested as I am." Keith mentioned that he sees the importance of dialogue and asserted that it makes the decision-making processes easier. He has noticed that when it is time to make difficult decisions, it is much easier for those involved because they have been engaged in continuous conversations already. He continued to say that dialogue helps them to think outside the box, "which is a hard thing for a lot of physicians to do."

To Joe, dialogue is important, and he stated that anytime you change a culture, you have to have consensus. He expressed strong feelings that if close cooperation and collaboration are not present in an organization, it will fail. Joe said, "Just about everything we do here is collaboration—from the point systems, to mealtimes, to sports programs, to classroom activities. Only by dialogue can we make these things happen smoothly." Dialogue is facilitated by Joe on a daily bases with the leadership team. He then would continue dialoguing through the day with members of his team. This continuous dialoguing contributed greatly to the team being able to make important decisions with relative ease. Joe stated, "I believe that dialogue is essential, and it is time consuming, but it's important and has to be done." He added, "But you can't let one person dominate the conversation; we can't sit in the office all day; we have to get out and do the work." Joe stated that he believes there is a connection between dialogue and the bottom line because you have to create an environment of honesty and communication in the organization. He asserted that when a tough decision has to be made, the relationship that has formed from the continuous dialogue allows the decisions that need to be made quickly to move much smoother.

Alma expressed the importance of dialogue and spoke about a company program last year called an environmental dialogue that reached out to 50 artists and leaders and asked for the participation of as many staff as possible. That experience showed her the power of dialogue. She stated that, now, when the company starts new programs, dialogue plays a major role in the process. Dialogue within the organization leads the company to new and incredible programs. She stated, "The dialogue led to the starting of an incredible new program, which was intended to help high school kids from disadvantaged communities and low-income families receive job training and internships in the arts." She continued to explain that the organization now has people banging down its doors seeking volunteer opportunities because that program has such a good reputation. As a result of the dialogue, the company was the first arts organization to participate in a grant from the government services in San Francisco.

While considering dialogue and the bottom line, Alma admitted that dialogue has been difficult in her current situation because she has had to make difficult decisions about programs and has had to lay off employees. So, at times, she has made choices between prolonged dialogue and the bottom line. According to Alma, even though difficult decisions have to be made and sometimes dialogue has to be cut short, she still has to treat the people she lays off with dignity. She said, "Basically, you have to look at the bottom line, and you can't keep supporting something that's not generating enough income."

All the situations presented above illustrate the trans-cultural leaders' ability to use dialogic principles to facilitate change within their organizations.

The trans-cultural leader's ability to lead above man made barriers of culture and move the many to one in vision, purpose and action is greatly influenced by the trans-cultural leader's understanding of culture as it applies to organizations and a myriad of other human applications, the leader's understanding of and their ability to draw from their life's experiences and the leader's aptitude for facilitating generative and strategic dialogue.

These abilities are manifested through the engagement of the Trans-Cultural leader's heart, mind, and soul.

The Heart, the Mind, and the Soul. After the interviews with the leaders, I used the information from my review of literature to develop an analytical framework. The literature review provided me with several characteristics of leaders who lead in multicultural environments (see Table 1) but also revealed that there is very little information on the type of leader behaviors necessary for leading in different organizational settings (Masoond et al., 2006). Therefore, I compiled the characteristics from the various sources in the literature review and grouped them into three different families—the Heart, the Mind, and the Soul. I chose these families because they speak of the parts of the person that some believe enables connection and engagement.

As mentioned earlier, the Heart is defined as the part of leaders that allows them to connect with themselves and others. The Mind is that part of leaders that is observant, discerning, and analytical. The Soul is the part of leaders that guides them through organizational life and allows them to guide others. Table 2 illustrates the three families and the corresponding characteristics found in the review of literature.

The Heart, the Mind, and the Soul Framework

Characteristic (s)	Family
- Accommodating - Community minded - Concerned with the common good - Culturally aware - Good sense of humor - Humanizing - Legitimizing - Relational - Transparent - Understands subordinates' needs	The Heart—*the part of leaders that allows them to connect with themselves and others.*
- Able to expand perspective, explore options, and create alternatives - Able to identify and eliminate hindrances to cultural inclusion - Able to suspend judgment, observe current group behavior, identify relevant information, and overcome ethnocentrism - Competent - Considers relevant moral issues - Culturally competent - Makes appropriate decisions - Mindful of the consequences his or her decisions have on all parties involved - Reflective	The Mind—*very astute observers, with keen discernment when it comes to their surroundings. They are analytical in their approach to their work and their lives.*
- A model citizen - Ability to motivate others - Culturally open - Delegates appropriately - Empowers others - Ethical - Facilitates the free flow of information - Mentors subordinates - Places group interests above his or her own - Principled - Promotes independent thinking in subordinates - Sincere interest in subordinates - Trustworthy	The Soul—*guides and allows leaders to steer others through organizational life. They are patient with themselves, their peers, and their subordinates.*

The characteristics listed above are not all inclusive, and a leader need not possess each and every one.

A good way to see a trans-cultural leader's heart, mind and soul in action is to ask those directly affected by the leader's approach. Therefore the following section will focus on the experiences of three of each of the transcultural leaders discussed above.

Heart, Mind and Soul in Action the Subordinates Experiences

Doug mentioned that he reports directly to Rony, and they have both scheduled and unscheduled communications. He commented that Rony's interactions with him have always been "scheduled, unscheduled, open, pleasant, and honest." Doug's overall perception of Rony is that he is a good solid leader. He reported that Rony does a very good job at helping him not to worry about things and encourages him to see the big picture in the scheme of things. Doug sees Rony as a person who is able to bring a sense of calm to the room. He recalled times when he would have "something on his mind" that he thought was a "very big problem," and, according to Doug, Rony would "let me know that in the big scheme of things, I probably need to let it go." He called Rony a visionary and one who is able to make his employees stretch. Doug pointed out that his leader's ability to respond calmly to difficult situations and to make others realize that it is not as difficult as they think are two of his major strengths. He commented on Rony's level of competence and stated, "I think that what he does well is his ability to keep his eye on the big picture and being a visionary for his company." In commenting on Rony's professional relationship with others, Doug stated that he believes Rony sees his job as helping other people perform better, and he approaches each individual differently. Doug said, "I think he tends to work one to one with folks in a way that does not humiliate others." Rony empowers his employees and allows them to have a voice in his organization. Doug sees Rony as a leader who "sees his job as making us better at what we do." This statement alludes to Rony's ability to show genuine concern for the betterment of his followers. According to Doug, Rony constantly tells everyone that they are all part of a team. Doug reported that Rony is able to involve others in the decision-making process. He stated, "Rony involves people in the decision-making process by moving gingerly and forcefully. He can act in different ways depending on the decision that has to be made and the people that are involved."

Doug admitted to a level of connection with Rony in many ways because Rony takes time to confide in him; and Doug noted that he feels as though Rony trusts him. Another reason for the connection is that Doug can see that Rony cares about the organization and the people who work there. His caring is shown through his actions when making hard decisions. He is very methodical; he does not rush, and he involves others in his decision-making process. After pointing out a way that Rony makes his decisions, Doug recalled the time when Rony decided to pursue the company in New York for patent infringements. He recalled how Rony was able to bring everyone on board and help them to feel at ease during this massive undertaking.

Doug said he believes that Rony is "honest, compassionate, caring, selfless, trustworthy and funny," which motivates him to perform at his best. He stated that Rony expects his subordinates to be free and to perform at their best because his company has over 500 employees, and the leaders in his company have to be able to navigate day-to-day operations and make the right decisions for running the company.

As the director of scientific affairs, Mark reported that he has very few formal interactions with Rony. He did admit, however, that Rony tends to stop him in the hall to ask him what is going on in his department and what course should be taken for specific issues. "So, overall, I'd say that our relationship is cordial and cooperative," he commented. Mark said he believes that Rony is certainly in tune with the mission to save lives and restore health to people and that Rony is a visionary who is able to impart vision to others. Mark said, "Rony does a good job at conveying the fact that he is very much behind the mission of this organization. And if you asked anyone in this organization if Rony cares about the donor family, they would say, 'Yes!'"

Mark pointed out that he sees Rony as a leader who allows experts in his company to be experts and encourages independent thinking. Mark exhibited a belief that Rony empowers his subordinates by holding them accountable and including them in the business of the business. Mark stated,

> He understands that we all want to be where the action is and not be out in left field or sitting on the bench. He has a lot of people who report to him, and we all welcome being held accountable, because he knows the buck stops with him and he takes responsibility for himself.

He gets things done in the leader/follower paradigm by holding people accountable. Mark commented that when Rony has to make difficult personnel choices, he knew that he could not "turn the cart too quickly, because that would've caused problems." Mark noticed that when Rony first arrived, he sat back and listened, assessed, and then made deliberate decisions. One decision that Mark remembered Rony making was that he decided to form an Institute of Regenerative Medicine in the organization. He had to decide how to go about forming such an institute and also how he could hire the needed experts. Mark recalled that Rony cast the vision, and others understood what he was talking about. His decision directly pointed to his ability to expand perspective as a trans-cultural leader. In thinking about the process that Rony had to take, Mark stated,

He first had an idea, and so he had to decide how he would bring someone here to carry out his vision. Therefore, he had to shepherd the hiring of the field expert in the area in order to get the input so he could put the idea out to others and helped them understand that regenerative medicine is necessary for this company.

Mark said he finds Rony to be conscientious, caring, respectful, intelligent, and curious. Rony provides freedom and autonomy for his employees, which allows them to perform at their best. Mark stated, "He provides that freedom by not being a micromanager and not being someone who has a list of objectives for you to complete and then comes around often and checks off boxes over and over again." The above quote by Mark shows that

Rony has an understanding of his subordinates' needs to feel worthwhile, encouraged, and motivated.

Robin, the director of donor family services, reported that he has worked for the company for 12 years and that he has a unique perspective on several leaders. He began our conversation about Rony's leadership ability by commenting on how often he meets with him to discuss issues about specific areas of leadership, in addition to his attendance to the biweekly Quick Intelligence (IQ) meetings. Robin's initial statement shows that he has noticed Rony's ability to facilitate the free flow of information. He indicated that he believes Rony brought good business acumen tempered with humaneness. Robin also recognizes that Rony is committed to "communication up and down the chain." He stated, "I think there is a regular effort through quarterly meetings and newsletters to facilitate effective communication." Robin noted that his role is unique because his department does not generate revenue but is very impressed that Rony believes that his department is very important.

Robin admitted that he rarely has seen Rony handling difficult situations; however, he has noticed the level of calm that Rony brings into a situation. He said, "Rony addresses situations attentively and intentionally. He does not make authoritative decisions unless he really feels like he's on to something." Robin also commented on Rony's ability to expand perspective, and, as an example, he stated, "Rony is very good at identifying the big-picture issues and defining what we need to focus on." Robin appreciates that Rony "seeks to generate ideas and helps others see the bigger picture."

Robin is very impressed with Rony's interactions with others around him. He notices that Rony is very attentive to donor families, and he has the ability to speak with people from all socioeconomic levels. Robin commented, with a smile on his face, "Rony has the ability to introduce himself and add to the conversations of many people and get them to open up to him in deep ways." Robin's acknowledgment of Rony's ability to interact well with others could indicate that this subordinate recognizes Rony's ability to be community minded. Rony is able to bring people together. Robin stated that Rony uses the QI meetings as a way to help his employees put plans together and set objectives. He also motivates others to work hard.

Robin said he feels connected with Rony because Rony understands the importance of his department. Robin asserted, "Rony just knows how important donor family services are to the culture of this institution, in terms of recognizing that all we do is based on compassionate decisions that organ and tissue donors make at the time of their loved one's death." The sense of connection is also fostered by Rony's leadership style. Robin called Rony a servant leader because Rony always states that he is there to help. Robin pointed out that Rony's style of leadership "definitely provides me with room to grow because he allows me to work without his micromanaging." Robin believes that Rony's leadership style certainly helps employees to perform at their best. He considers that Rony is operating with his heart, his soul, and his intellect.

Each of Rony's subordinates represented a different part of the respondent's organization with distinctly differing functions and focuses. However, their responses indicated that Rony is able to take the specific cultures of each department and move them towards purposeful cooperative action by providing space for regular meetings between departments and communicating the need to pursue litigation in order to protect the company's interests.

The following is a summary of Keith's subordinates' descriptions of his leadership style Peggy was working for Keith in several different capacities at the time of the interview. Her perception of Keith was that he is a very positive leader and a strong visionary. She stated, "He sometimes sees things that others can't see, and he is not one to wait; he makes things happen." Peggy explained that the foundation, for which she is a board member, focuses on providing everyday people with tools they need to reach their health goals.

Peggy said that Keith responds to difficult situations by remaining calm. She stated that it seems like the more excited and frantic a situation becomes, the calmer Keith gets. She commented that she believes Keith's faith helps keep him centered. According to Peggy, Keith has a good relationship with his employees because he lets them know his expectations and he actually listens to them. He involves others in the decision-making process, but he asks that people remain respectful.

Peggy commented that Keith has always been interested in the community and helping people who are less fortunate. According to Peggy, Keith is interested in creating community in his company as well. His ability to consider relevant issues was alluded to in her recollection of her leader's reasons for starting the PLLC. He saw the change in healthcare coming and thought it was unacceptable that small practices were seemly getting chewed up. Keith understood the consequences that would result by his actions, and Peggy said, "He spoke to physicians of smaller practices and developed a network, thereby solidifying their power and adding more bargaining power when it comes to contracts and healthcare for employees." The positive consequences included solidified power and greater bargaining ability for those in the PLLC. This move empowered not only those who joined but their employees as well.

Keith's ability to lead others with differences toward a common goal is seen in the forming of the PLLC. Peggy stated that, initially, many physicians did not accept Keith's vision, but, as the climate continued to change, more physicians joined his organization. Peggy stated, "He explained to them what he saw in the future and gave them some examples. He started to speak to people individually and have many one-on-one conversations with them, and then he would meet with everyone as a group and share his vision." Resistance came because many of his colleagues wanted to maintain their autonomy, but, when they started to see a trend of referrals decreasing for their practices because parent organizations only wanted physicians and other professionals to refer to the physicians and other professionals within the parent company's system, they realized that Keith's idea was a good alternative to going out of business.

Peggy pointed out that she sees Keith as a very independent thinker, a man who is a visionary, as well as a compassionate and caring person. She stated that her leader provides her with space to grow because he allows her to do her job and he does not micromanage. She stated, "He doesn't micromanage me, and if I come to one of the physicians and other professionals and tell them something about a change that needs to happen, he empowers me to do what I must do in order to get the job done."

Keith's executive assistant, Flora considers herself to be Keith's "right-hand woman." She reported that she takes care of everything for him, which includes all of his business ventures. She stated that Keith does many things well, but one of his strengths is his ability to run his business ventures while maintaining a vibrant cardiology practice. She also commented on Keith's ability to expand perspective and explore options. She said she believes that "he researches and discusses his issues with others and then calmly makes a decision based on the facts that he found in his research."

Flora stated that Keith is very professional and does not lead by intimidation; he leads because people respect him. Flora said, "Keith tends to delegate and is not authoritarian; he has a knack for being able to hire good staff and is very much in tune with what his vision is." Flora's statements painted a picture of a leader who is able to delegate appropriately and empower his subordinates. According to Flora, he is very relational. She supported this comment by saying, "Through the course of his years in practice, he made a variety of relationships. It is all about relationships." Flora attributes Keith's success to his ability to form relationships with others, which allows him to "lead his people by respecting them."

Flora explained that she feels a level of connection with Keith because of his level of professionalism, and she said she believes he is a good guy by showing he cares. His caring demeanor allows him to approach difficult decisions in a non-reactionary way. He tends to discuss decisions with others after he has thought about them for a while, and when he makes decisions, he is very purposeful in his actions. Flora asserted, "He engages his heart and his brain."

Flora also attributed Keith's success to his longevity in his field. He has developed and has maintained many relationships throughout the course of his career, and Flora suggested that she understands relationships are very important to Keith. Flora noted that Keith is able to foster such relationships and be very successful in his ventures because he is hard working, ethical, respectful, and visionary. When asked how Keith has allowed Flora to perform at her best, she stated, "He provides me the space to perform at my best by keeping an open mind and even allowing me to make suggestions to improve things."

Sam, one of Keith's physician assistants in his cardiology practice, stated that his overall perception of Keith as a leader is that he is "the best boss I've had in my entire working career." He described Keith as a very professional, intelligent, and thoughtful person. According to Sam, Keith does just about everything well, and he provides Sam with every opportunity to grow. Sam presented a picture of his leader as a very competent man. He said, "It seems like Keith has enough experience that he automatically knows how to resolve any problem that he is presented with." When asked about Keith's ability to handle stressful situations, Sam stated that he has noticed that Keith is very level headed, relaxed and calm, and it seems that he has a solution always readily at hand. Keith is the "boss" and that certain boundaries must be maintained. Sam commented,

> Keith's relationship with others who work for him is that he is the boss, but he doesn't have to say it; my professional opinion is that he's able to maintain the boundaries between boss and employee because he cares about his employees and he allows us to talk openly and even joke around, but we understand that there is a line that we can't cross.

Sam said he believes Keith gets things done by not micromanaging but by making sure that each employee understands his or her responsibilities.

Sam emphatically stated that he feels a level of connection with Keith because he "has been in the workforce since he was 17 years old and has had several careers, and Keith is the most compassionate and understanding boss to work for." He attributed his boss's success to Keith's ability to stay very current with the issues and his ability to make decisions based on the current economic and social climate. He noted that Keith has managed to build a strong level of trust with his employees by always being honest and straightforward.

Sam showed a high level of confidence in his ability to carry out his job because, "Keith has given me very good opportunities to grow, learn, and increase my skills in his company." Sam certainly looked and acted like an empowered subordinate because he believes Keith has a sincere interest in his subordinates. He said, "If I have any concerns or problems, he is always there to assist me, even if I have a personal problem."

The following section is a summary of Joe's subordinates' descriptions of his leadership style.

Fred, the program manager for the facility's behavior support program, reflected a belief that Joe is very patient and thoughtful and does several things well, such as taking feedback from his staff and giving good advice. According to Fred, Joe uses his ability to empower his subordinates to improve the facility. He has seen Joe respond to difficult situations by giving a lot of thought before making decisions. Fred stated, "He takes the time to see what is the best and safest way to do things. I have never seen him act out of character. He has never taken matters into his own hands; he always consults others." Fred stated that Joe has good relationships with everybody he contacts because "he is comfortable to be around and he knows how to make people feel at ease around him." Joe gets things done by delegating and not micromanaging. Joe's leadership style allows for Fred to feel a level of connection to him. Fred added that Joe has compassion and genuine concern for others in the facility. It appears to Fred that Joe is not only concerned with his personal success but the success of all his subordinates as well.

Fred recognized that Joe's concern for others and his high level of professionalism allow his employees to not feel slighted or disrespected. Even when he had to let go a person in the management team, Joe advocated for that person to get a job in another part of the company.

Fred mentioned that Joe is able to delegate appropriately and he "coaches along the way and points out your weak points and strong points but he does not micromanage. This approach to leadership empowers others and allows them to perform at their best," Fred asserted. Joe's ability to build consensus by getting people from differing professional cultures to work together was evident to Fred during Joe's implementation of the new behavior modification program, which was called the Matrix. Implementation of the program required countless hours of training, and, according to Fred, "Joe allowed us to bounce ideas around and make changes to the program as we saw fit." Fred finds it encouraging that Joe "takes feedback from his staff and provides excellent feedback in return." This statement alludes to Joe's willingness to mentor subordinates. Fred's statement pointed to Joe's humanizing nature; he said, "Joe makes everyone who comes into contact with him feel comfortable, and he knows how to communicate without making other people feel inferior." Fred concluded his comments about the behavioral modification program by stating, "Once Joe felt comfortable with what we had concluded, he allowed the management team to continue on with implementation."

Fred ascribed to Joe the following characteristics: caring, contemplative, professional, experienced, and grounded. He continued by stating that Joe provides him the freedom to perform at his best by not micromanaging and allows him to be creative at the way he approaches his work. Fred also stated that Joe is a "very professional, up-front, and honest man." He followed by stating that Joe is very patient, thoughtful, and "considerate of all staff as well as residents."

Terry, the program manager for the facility's project right track program, explained that Joe is a "systems kind of guy" because he sees things systematically and insists that his management team works hard and smart. Terry expressed the thought that Joe does several things well, but Terry particularly focused on Joe's ability to not be a dictator and actually show concern for those who work for him. Terry expressed a belief that Joe is a fair employer and has integrity, and he stated, "He comes across as a very likable person, and I think other people respect Joe because he's very personable and he gets things done by being able to delegate and lead by example." Terry commented that Joe is there for his employees, and he never makes them feel like they are bothering him; that is why Terry feels a level of connection to him.

Terry commented that he believes Joe "is able to see things from many perspectives and is willing to take everyone's feedback." which shows Joe's potential to expand perspective. Terry talked about a time when Joe had to review a packet for a possible admission into the program. Terry stated that a decision to admit a person can be very difficult, and he noticed that Joe did not make a hasty decision but took the time to speak with the clinical director before he made a decision. Terry pointed out that Joe has the ability to deal with difficult decisions by being mindful.

In discussing a decision that Joe made to lead the organization in a different direction, Terry stated that the implementation of the Matrix program required that he would get many people involved. There were many discussions about the implementation, and Joe listened to everyone's input. Terry stated, "I saw Joe as more of a facilitator during the process." Terry was very impressed by Joe's ability to allow everyone to have a voice and to be heard in the organization.

Terry ascribed the following characteristics to Joe: kind, business oriented, well driven, and compassionate. Joe is able to see things from many perspectives, and that is what motivates Terry to perform at his highest level. In conclusion, Terry stated, "He gives me the opportunity to be successful, and he does not micromanage me."

Spence, the medical director of the facility, commented that Joe presents himself in a supportive and collegial manner. He noted that Joe's style of administration is like that of a coach by providing supportive leadership and guidance to a majority of those who report to him, and he also interfaces well with the various professional and departmental levels throughout the organization.

Spence has noticed that Joe's relationship with others who work for him is quite good and that he gets things done by utilizing his communication skills in explaining the reasons for his decisions and sharing his perception of certain things in the organization. Spence stated that he appreciates Joe's situation and respects the struggles that he has to contend with in order to carry out his job. Joe does a good job of sharing his thoughts and the reasons for his decisions. Spence stated that he is not included in many of the decision-making discussions but has noticed that Joe often moves out among the staff and the residents to gather their input and to provide support, which indicates that Spence believes that Joe's leadership style shows that he has a sincere interest in his followers. According to Spence, Joe has the ability to expand perspective and explore options by "explaining the reason for his decisions and sharing how he perceives certain things in the organization." He also shares his perspective about situations with others within the organization, regardless of their position. Spence indicated that he believes Joe is honest, supportive, and caring, and has a genuine desire to help others and to thereby help the facility.

The following is a summary of Alma's subordinates' descriptions of her leadership style. Ellen, the executive director of the Sacramento office, had been employed by the organization for 14 years at the time of the interview. Ellen had known Alma for several years and said she believes they have a close relationship. Her office is "a long way from San Francisco," and she communicates with Alma mainly on the phone and via e-mail. Ellen stated that Alma is a very smart woman and that she has many good ideas. Ellen added, "Alma can lead well in difficult situations because she can break them down and make the right decisions. Alma handles most difficult situations by getting involved." Ellen recalled a time when she had to meet with the Sacramento Board of Supervisors, which was very stressful for her. The Sacramento office had to make a presentation to the County Board to show what the program could offer. Ellen stated that she was very new to the job and to the program, and she had to contact her leader for assistance. Alma provided Ellen with the information and direction she needed, and Alma also decided to go to Sacramento to support Ellen. She informed Ellen that she needed to gather several people to speak on behalf of the organization and follow with her presentation. Ellen appreciated the support and encouragement that Alma provided.

Ellen said she believes that Alma has a hands-off approach when it comes to leadership. Ellen feels empowered by Alma because Alma promotes independent thinking and has an understanding that she needs to feel engaged and worthwhile. Ellen stated, "I have to say that I have a really great working relationship with Alma, primarily because she trusts me to do what I need to do to get the job done. I feel like she has confidence in my ability." Alma has always been available and very willing to talk to Ellen. Ellen feels a level of connection to Alma because they have known each other for several years; she said she feels like Alma is a friend and tends to include others in her decision-making processes. Ellen spoke about a time when a long-time staff member resigned, and Alma had to fill the position. It was well within Alma's rights to hire someone without consulting others; however, she sought the input of other people because it would involve changing the direction for the organization in some way. Ellen said, "She was very willing to discuss this with us and with me."

According to Ellen, Alma works with people one at a time; she gives them individual attention, and she likes to build coalitions through individual relationships. Ellen remembered a time when Alma wanted to take the company in a new direction by creating a youth program. There was a lot of resistance to add such a program, but she started talking to each person who resisted the idea and attempted to show the benefits of going in that direction. She shared that the benefits were not just economic but also that it was socially responsible to do such things for children.

Ellen finds Alma to be smart, attentive, accessible, and inclusive. Ellen considers herself to be the type of person who "could not work with someone looking over my shoulder," And for that reason, Ellen expressed satisfaction that Alma has the management style that allows Ellen to be free to do what she thinks is best for the Sacramento office. Ellen added, "That approach allows me to be creative and innovative."

As program director, Jill reports directly to Alma. Jill's overall perception of Alma is that she is a very inspiring and energetic leader. She also provided input concerning Alma's ability to be community minded and strong. She stated that Alma is always willing to do whatever she needs to do to provide service to people, regardless of their level of income. Jill expressed a belief that Alma does several things well; she is especially appreciative of Alma's optimism and ability to motivate others. Jill stated, "She's always keeping hope alive." Jill said that Alma handles difficult situations by "stepping up to the plate." She provided an example of a time when a program that Alma was very connected to was about to be defunded. Alma spent a small amount of time being disappointed,

The Transcultural Leader, Leading the Way to PCA

but, afterwards, she started strategizing about how to move beyond the disappointing situation.

"Alma has a good relationship with others who work for her because she's very cordial, pleasant, and warm," said Jill. She observed that Alma gets things done in the follower/leader paradigm because she is a good delegator, and she provides room for her followers to express themselves. Jill pointed out that Alma rarely micromanages; however, there have been times when an individual had to receive more of Alma's attention in order to be helped with a particular project. Alma was always ready to step back and allow her followers to be creative. Alma's leadership style and concern for her employees allowed Jill to feel a level of connection with her. Jill said, "She's been very personally supportive as well as professionally supportive of me, and she knows my family, and she is sort of like an extended family."

According to Jill, Alma has had to make some difficult decisions when it comes to the viability of a certain part of the organization. Jill reported that Alma has the ability to build consensus and encourage cooperation. She gave an example of the times when Alma is working on fundraising events: "Not everyone works directly on the project, but she will always engage us and allow us to feel like we're part of the project, which inspires everyone to be creative in the way that they can contribute." Jill described Alma as a visionary, engaging, and compassionate leader. She said that Alma provides the freedom for her to perform at her best by not being a micromanager. She added, "Alma is interested in delegating and seeing you perform at your best; she's not interested in finding fault with you, she is only interested in making suggestions when necessary and supporting you and encouraging you."

Karla had been employed by Alma's organization for approximately 2½ years and at the time of the interview was an associate director. She expressed a belief that Alma is very collaborative and cooperative in her leadership style. Karla stated, "She is open for your input and your ideas about the office; she's very open to new ideas that could move the organization in positive directions." Karla stated that Alma is always open to facilitating and handles tough situations in positive ways. She noticed that Alma is always interested in hearing the employees' perspectives.

It has been Karla's experience that Alma is very accessible, and she gets things done in the organization through collaboration, being proactive, and always willing to "do whatever it takes." Karla has noticed that Alma is always "in work mode and is very good at delegating and tapping into each individual's talents and abilities." Karla said she feels a connection with her leader on both personal and professional levels. She attributed the connection to Alma's accessibility.

Karla recalled a situation when one of the offices was going through many changes, and Alma had to make a difficult choice. Karla observed Alma taking the time to think the whole process through and receive input from other employees. According to Karla, Alma is always encouraging all offices to work together and to coordinate their efforts. Karla asserted, "Alma always encourages us to speak with our counterparts in the other offices so we can build relationships."

Karla said that Alma is "wise, passionate, a visionary, understanding, and nurturing." She also said that Alma provides her the freedom to perform at her best by letting her set her own schedule, which gives her the flexibility to allow her to do her job. Karla acknowledged that Alma's leadership approach allows Karla to be at her best when she is in the office because she knows that her family issues are taken care of and she is not distracted.

V

Putting it all together

The above section provided a descriptive view of the four trans-cultural leaders I chose for this book and subordinates who worked with them. The descriptions presented by the participants need to be viewed in relation to their backdrop. The backdrop that surrounds the phenomenon in question (i.e., leading trans-culturally) allows it to be seen clearly from different vantage points. As previously mentioned, the backdrop in this book that was common to all these leaders was that they lead in organizations that exist in a nation that has historically experienced being fractured by race, gender, class, sex, profession, and faith. Different vantage points were provided by each individual participant's description of the phenomena, allowing the phenomena of trans-cultural leadership to be observed through their stories and reflections. I referred to Table 2, which lists the characteristics of a trans-cultural leader, and I also used the categorizations of the Heart, the Mind, and the Soul listed to tag each relevant statement provided by the participants.

Table 2 was used as an analytical framework because the literature review contained a substantial amount of valuable information that described the characteristics of effective leaders. The framework allowed me to organize the characteristics provided by the many different authors referred to earlier and categorize them according to three families (the Heart, the Mind, and the Soul). The framework also provided a standard scale in which to analyze the comments provided by the leaders and their subordinates. The three families mentioned above were chosen because I presented four leaders' experiences interacting in their worlds. In order to fully engage, people must bring all of who they are to the encounter; therefore, the Heart, the Mind, and the Soul represent the complete person as they "turn to" (Buber, 1970) the phenomena of leading trans-culturally.

My interactions with the leaders and their subordinates provided a wealth of insight from various people with different perspectives of the phenomena in question. The analysis presents a description of leading trans-culturally from each leader within the context of his or her organization coupled with the descriptions of the leader's three subordinates. Following that, it compares the leader's descriptions with each other and shows overarching themes within the descriptions.

Table 3 illustrates the categorizations of the statements provided by the leaders pertaining to their experiences leading trans-culturally. The table also provides the reader with an illustration of the subordinates' observations.

Tran-cultural leaders' Heart, Mind, and Soul and Subordinates' Observations

Family	Leaders' Characteristic With Number of Times Alluded To	Subordinates' Observations of Leaders' Characteristics With Number of Times Alluded To
Heart	<ul><li>Culturally aware (8)</li><li>Community minded (7)</li><li>Relational (4)</li><li>Transparent (4)</li><li>Concerned with the common good (3)</li><li>Humanizing (3)</li><li>Accommodating (2)</li><li>Legitimizing (2)</li><li>Good sense of humor (1)</li><li>Understands subordinates' needs (1)</li></ul>	<ul><li>Relational (17)</li><li>Understands subordinates' needs (10)</li><li>Humanizing (9)</li><li>Community minded (5)</li><li>Legitimizing (4)</li><li>Culturally aware (2)</li><li>Accommodating (1)</li><li>Good sense of humor (1)</li><li>Transparent (1)</li></ul>
Mind	<ul><li>Culturally competent (5)</li><li>Able to expand perspective, explore options, create alternatives (4)</li><li>Able to identify and eliminate hindrances to cultural inclusion (4)</li><li>Considers relevant moral issues (3)</li><li>Mindful of the consequences his or her decisions have on all parties involved (3)</li><li>Reflective (3)</li><li>Able to suspend judgment, observe current group behavior, identify relevant information, and overcome ethnocentrism (2)</li><li>Makes appropriate decisions (2)</li></ul>	<ul><li>Competent (17)</li><li>Able to expand perspective, explore options, create alternatives (11)</li><li>Makes appropriate decisions (7)</li><li>Able to identify and eliminate hindrances to cultural inclusion (5)</li><li>Able to suspend judgment, observe current group behavior, identify relevant information, and overcome ethnocentrism (2)</li><li>Reflective (2)</li><li>Considers relevant moral issues (1)</li><li>Mindful of the consequences his or her decisions have on all parties involved (1)</li></ul>
Soul	<ul><li>Facilitates the free flow of information (5)</li><li>Ability to motivate others (4)</li><li>Culturally open (4)</li><li>Empowers others (4)</li><li>Places group interests above his or her own (4)</li><li>Trustworthy (2)</li><li>Promotes independent thinking in subordinates (1)</li><li>Sincere interest in subordinates (1)</li></ul>	<ul><li>Empowers others (17)</li><li>Sincere interest in subordinates (13)</li><li>Ability to motivate others (9)</li><li>Delegates appropriately (7)</li><li>Trustworthy (6)</li><li>Mentors subordinates (5)</li><li>Promotes independent thinking in subordinates (5)</li><li>Facilitates the free flow of information (4)</li><li>Places group interests above his or her own (3)</li><li>Ethical (1)</li><li>Principled (1)</li></ul>

The following is an analysis of the characteristics exuded by the Trans-cultural leaders' and alluded to by the subordinates' descriptions of leading trans-culturally in multicultural environments.

Analysis of Characteristics

The statements provided by the trans-cultural leaders and their subordinates provided valuable insight into the experiences of both the trans-cultural leaders and their followers' perceptions of their leaders' trans-cultural leadership. The following analysis brings to the forefront the themes that emerged from the comments of the leaders and the subordinates. I present the percentile of the most prevalent comments provided by the participants not in an attempt to quantify the participants' experiences but in order to aid in the presentation of the data.

The leaders made 86 comments that fell within the Heart, the Mind, and the Soul of the trans-cultural leadership experience. Forty-one percent of the comments provided by the leaders fell into the Heart family, 30% of the comments fell into the Mind family, and 29% of the comments fell into the Soul family.

The leaders' comments concerning their ability to connect with themselves and others were prevalent during our conversations, as evidenced by the previous percentage breakdown. The leaders' comments alluding to cultural awareness accounted for 23% of the total comments within the Heart family, followed closely by 20% of the comments concerning community mindedness. The leaders' comments concerning transparency and being relational both accounted for 11% of the Heart family comments, respectively.

The Mind and the Soul families were one percentage point apart, with the leaders' statements alluding to cultural competence, which was 19% of the Mind family, and facilitation of the free flow of information, which was

20% of the Soul family, topping the lists. Following closely behind within the Mind family at 15% each were the leaders' comments showing their ability to expand perspective, explore options, and create alternatives, and their comments concerning their ability to identify and eliminate hindrances to cultural inclusion. The leaders' comments showing their ability to motivate and empower others, being culturally open, and placing other interests above their own each individually accounted for 16% of the Soul family.

The subordinates' comments concerning their perception of their leaders' trans-cultural leadership was slightly different, with 43% their 167 comments falling into the Soul family. The Heart family accounted for 30% of the comments, and the Mind family accounted for 28% of the comments provided by the subordinates.

Within the Soul family of the subordinates' comments, 24% of the comments described their leaders' ability to empower them, and 18% of the comments showed a belief that their leaders have a sincere interest in them. Thirteen percent of their comments pointed towards their leaders' ability to motivate them.

The Heart family's number one category was the subordinates' descriptions pointing to their leaders' ability to be relational, which accounted for 31% of their statements. The subordinates also made statements that showed that they believe their leaders understand their needs, which was 20% of their comments.

The Mind family included the subordinates' beliefs that their leaders were competent at their jobs, which accounted for 37% of the statements in that family. They also made comments that showed that they believe their leaders have the ability to expand perspective, explore options, and create alternatives, which accounted for 25% of their comments.

These results show that these leaders utilize the "Heart of trans-cultural leadership" to lead in their multicultural organizations more than the other families. As stated earlier, this is the part of the leaders that allows them to connect to themselves and others, which calls for them to be aware of their cultures and the cultures of those people they lead. The leaders showed an interest in the communities in which they live and work. They all made comments that demonstrated their ability to be relational and transparent during the interviews. The "Mind of trans-cultural leadership" is the second most used family within the matrix, with the "Soul of trans-cultural leadership" having only one percentage point difference.

The Mind refers to the part of leaders that analyzes situations and the part of leaders that has a keen discernment regarding their surroundings. The leaders provided comments that pointed to their cultural competence and their abilities to expand perspective, explore options, and create alternatives. The Soul of trans-cultural leaders refers to the part of the leaders that guides them through organizational life and allows them to guide others through organizational life. At the top of the list for the Soul family is the leaders' ability to facilitate the free flow of information. Each leader spoke about providing a place for the flow of information, which is filled with dialogic concepts.

The leaders' ability to engage the Heart, the Mind, and the Soul enables them to create an environment conducive for purposeful cooperative action within a multicultural landscape. The leaders' subordinates made the most comments that alluded to the "Soul of trans-cultural leadership." As the leaders activate their "hearts" by being aware of the cultures around them, by showing concern for the communities within and without the organization, by being transparent and relational, and by allowing their subordinates to feel empowered, subordinates are motivated because their leaders are sincerely interested in them.

Each subordinate saw his or her leader as being relational and understanding, which falls under the Heart family. The Heart family accounted for the second highest amount of comments provided by the subordinates as they described their leaders' leadership. Lastly, the leaders were all seen as people who are good at what they do and very capable; as seen in the most alluded to code within the Mind family, which is associated with having competence to carry out their work in a way that meets the expectations others hold of the person and the position.

This analysis shows that the four leaders in this book intentionally lead through their cultural awareness and knowledge and their ability to develop and attend to their relationships with others. As a result, those who report to them recognize the value of their relationships with their leaders and feel empowered and motivated to perform their work through the extension of trust and delegation.

This chapter provided a view of four trans-cultural leaders through their own reflections on their leadership and through the reflections of their subordinates. The following chapter summarizes the study, answers the questions of the study, and provides possible future studies.

The journey towards understanding the experiences of trans-cultural leaders was stimulated by a research practicum class and my first consulting job. I was interested in understanding the life-giving factors of a multicultural church in Northern California when it functioned at its best. The research showed that the parishioners of that church placed the utmost importance on their relationships with God and believed their those relationships greatly affected their views of themselves. The parishioners' relationships with God allowed them to be able to focus on forming deep, meaningful relationships with each other. The multicultural environment was fostered by relationships—relationships with God, with their pastor, and with each other. Several factors combined to make the church what it was, and, upon closer analysis, I found that the life-giving factors that made the church a haven of multicultural interactions was facilitated by the senior pastor. This observation appeared to be validated by the departure of the senior pastor and the installation of a new pastor. The church slowly started to change from a multicultural haven to a monocultural organization.

My journey to understand the experiences of the trans-cultural leader also led me to my first consulting job with SRC. I realized that the president and CEO of the corporation was the driving force behind leading the people of different cultures, races, and disciplines into one purpose, vision, and action. The president and CEO managed to move his company from a small minority-owned majority African-American business to a successful multicultural support services business fulfilling multimillion-dollar contracts for the federal government at various locations throughout the country. After meeting the trans-cultural leaders in both venues—the church and SRC—I decided to embark on this journey to understand the "makeup" of such a leader.

I intended to describe the experiences of trans-cultural leaders as they lead people of different cultures toward purposeful cooperative action. I chose to phenomenologically look at the experience by starting with my Epoche, which is the suspension of beliefs. I set aside my prejudgments, ideas, and thoughts about how I think the phenomenon should be which is that in order for a person to lead in a multicultural environment, he or she must have a firm grasp of the concepts of culture and must be able to create an environment where dialogue can abound. The release of my judgment led me on a journey through the literature on trans-cultural leadership. I first sought to understand the historical perspective on leadership, followed by a search to understand the characteristics of such leaders. The search allowed me to identify several characteristics that could apply to a trans-cultural leader. I divided the characteristics into three categories: the Heart, the Mind, and the Soul. Following the categorizing of the characteristics of a trans-cultural leader, I set out to define culture and dialogue. In my search, I found that culture is an evolutionary manifestation guided by group members' interactions with their environments and with each other, where dialogue is ever flowing; yet, at times, it is a deliberate means by which others can gain understanding between themselves and their environments.

The next step was to find trans-cultural leaders to interview. I found four leaders who were willing to participate, along with 12 subordinates who were willing to give their perceptions of their leaders. The interviews proved to be very fruitful and helpful in my journey towards understanding the experiences of four trans-cultural leaders. The information gathered indicated that trans-cultural leaders lead by fostering connection; nurturing healthy relationships; facilitating communication; empowering others; identifying hindrances to cultural inclusion; and being culturally competent, culturally aware, culturally open, and community minded. The next section is a culmination of the leaders' experiences.

Culmination of trans-cultural characteristics.

The trans-cultural leader has a difficult but exciting job. He or she must know how to tap into his or her Heart, Mind, and Soul in order to lead in the 21st century, where borders that separate countries, cultures, and people are becoming more porous. It is of the utmost importance that leaders create environments of inclusion in organizations and communities.

As President Obama (2009) stated in his inauguration address, "Our patchwork heritage is a strength, not a weakness." Patchwork infers the maintenance of individuality with unity of purpose. In the case of the patchwork quilt, each piece is a different size, texture, and strength, but the common purpose could be to provide warmth, to preserve history, or to provide ascetic beauty.

The trans-cultural leader could be seen as the thread used to connect the pieces together. The thread must have certain characteristics that combine to help the quilt as a whole fulfill its purpose, and the leaders in this study showed certain characteristics in their descriptions of their experiences leading trans-culturally.

The following is a presentation of the major themes that emerged during the interviews as they pertained to the leaders' experiences leading trans-culturally. The interview questions were fashioned utilizing the information gathered in the literature review concerning the positive characteristics of a leader. The themes generated from the interviews fit neatly in the Heart, the Mind, and the Soul framework; however, I admit that another researcher looking at this particular phenomenon through the lens of his or her life experiences may have presented the emergent themes utilizing a different framework.

The Heart of trans-cultural leadership. There is a need to connect with self and others in the pursuit of leading trans-culturally. The prevailing theme in this study of leading trans-culturally is to be culturally aware. Connection calls for leaders to be aware of the evolving cultural story of those around them (Schein, 1996). A leader must be aware of the symbols, heroes, and values of each of the pieces of his or her organizational quilt (Hofstede & Hofstede, 2005). Williams (2007) pointed out that cultures can be seen as institutions and studied because they are visible and alive. Being culturally aware does not only lend itself to being aware of others but also calls for the leader to be aware of his or her own culture. A good understanding of how group members see themselves and others in relation to their environments is essential to leading trans-culturally (Triandis, 2003).

The trans-cultural leader leads by being community minded. His or her views are not solely focused on the "four walls" of the organization but are concerned with the symbiotic relationship with the community. The "social contract" spoken of by Ciulla (1998) between the leader and the follower is expanded to be between the organization and the community; the trans-cultural leader sees the organization as providing something beneficial to the community, not just taking from the community in which the organization exists.

Trans-cultural leaders not only connect with self and others but are also able to be very astute observers and able to discern and analyze organizational and life circumstances, which falls under the "Mind" of the trans-cultural leader.

The Mind of trans-cultural leadership. The trans-cultural leader leads by being able to expand perspective, explore options, and create alternatives. This type of leader is able to see the happenings within his or her organization or community from a view which allows the leader to create an environment of inclusiveness and overcome his or her own self-deception and bias about situations. This stance facilitates the creation of alternatives (Swanson, 2004). These leaders are able to eliminate hindrances to cultural inclusion by helping subordinates move past categorizations and stereotypes in order to focus on similarities.

Coffey and Tombari (2005) posited that leaders who create culturally inclusive environments are able to commit to continuous learning and improvement, which leads to increased ability to identifying and eliminating hurdles of inclusion.

The next section discusses the fact that leaders' ability to navigate through organizational life and guide others requires patience with themselves, with their peers, and with their subordinates, which is referred to as the Soul of trans-cultural leadership.

The Soul of trans-cultural leadership. Trans-cultural leaders are able to facilitate the free flow of information. These leaders understand that sustained dialogue adds to the inclusive environment of their organizations. A trans-cultural leader creates the place for open and free communication throughout his or her organization. Dialogue plays a major part in inclusion. It is akin to Buber's (1970) approach to dialogue where people are asked to "turn to" each other. The other department, section, or person does not fully "become" until there is a "turning." The trans-cultural leader is able to facilitate this dialogic process by understanding when the dialogue must become strategic while maintaining the perpetually turning and ever-flowing generative dialogue. Banathy and Jenlink (2005) pointed out that dialogue is something that can happen over several minutes or years and that it is basically a relationship we create and sustain.

The trans-cultural leader creates relationships within the organization or community that make purposeful cooperative action possible. Those relationships are created by impromptu dialogic encounters or by planned, expanded dialogic meetings, which appears to create a circle of communication and collaboration. Such leaders are able to acknowledge others as equals and understand that what he or she knows is only increased and augmented by others (Wheatley, 2002).

VI

Trans-Cultural Leader in Light of the Literature

A phenomenological approach seeks to listen to what is being said about a topic and then looks at the phenomena to see if what has been said is true. Brown's (2007) book provided several techniques that a trans-cultural leader should use in this multicultural environment because "business is conducted across national borders by parties whose cultural values and customs are dramatically different" (p. 6). Brown presented the idea that trans-cultural leaders should know how to communicate well, build relationships, mentor, have executive presence, build teams, set goals, and make decisions. His assertions were all substantiated by the results found in this book, as all the leaders and their subordinates referred to each of Brown's (2007) attributes. The only difference is that all these leaders are domestic leaders, with only one having an office outside the United States. This book shows that the attributes lauded by Brown are just as essential for the domestic leader, especially because this country is made up of people from all over the world. As stated earlier, we in this country have the benefit of being the recipients of some of the world's most ambitious and capable immigrants (Simons et al., 1993). It appears that the human experience and the needs presented in Maslow's (1943) hierarchy of needs could be universal and be used as the foundation on which to build a trans-cultural approach to leadership. Along the same vein is Wubbolding's (1988) assertion that the needs for belonging are manifested in society, work, and family and transcends the barriers placed by culture.

All of the leaders in this book spoke about issues that showed they were considering the relevant moral issues about their particular situation. Ciulla (1998) pointed out that ethics should be embedded in leadership, which was manifested throughout the responses of both the leaders and their subordinates. The themes that surfaced during the study showed that the leaders' overall experiences at leading trans-culturally included them being "good" both at their jobs and being morally competent. When their subordinates were asked what they thought their leaders do well, before they gave a particular answer a majority responded with a statement that acknowledged their leaders do most things well. That particular stance taken by most of the employees shows that they believe their leaders to be competent at most things.

The responses show that there is a level of connection between effective leaders and their followers, as seen in a subordinate's description of Alma's relationships. She stated that Alma was very personally supportive of her and seems like a part of the family, which shows a level of connection. The relationships did appear to be symbiotic, in that the leader's ability to help his or her followers navigate through organizational life, as shown by 96 total comments that fell within the Soul category (Table 8), gave the leader empowered, motivated subordinates. The leaders' comments about their experiences leading trans-culturally indicates that they present themselves as leaders who have genuine concern for those they lead and would not violate the "social contract" spoken of by Ciulla (1998). The trans-cultural leaders in the study are not interested in leading by using Ciulla's (1998) "Bogus Empowerment," which has at its foundation in dishonesty and deceit. The leaders presented in this study demonstrated that they value honesty and were called honest by their subordinates.

Campbell's (1990) work in which he studied the mythologies of many different cultures to find themes concerning the development of leaders, presented in Stech's (2009) paper, provided a list of stages that leaders go through to become the leaders they are. The gist of his paper is that leaders trained in the conventional methods are taught to not rely on their cultural pasts in order to conform to the "normal" tenets of leadership. It appears that the trans-cultural leaders in this study were able to be true to their cultures from which they came while recognizing and valuing the cultures they lead. The leaders in this study had been trained in the "conventional" way, which has it merits and they accredit for their entry into their positions. Yet, they were able to draw on the life experiences of their journeys toward becoming trans-cultural; the leaders all had comments that demonstrated their cultural awareness, openness, and competence. They also admitted to being influenced by their life experiences while leading trans-culturally. It appears that being able to master the worlds of vision, dreams, and ideas, and the worlds of human needs, conflicts, and limitations presented by Stech, was a natural occurrence for the participant leaders.

The concepts presented previously in this study concerning the characteristics of a trans-cultural leader were compiled into Table 1 and grouped into categories that I have called families. As mentioned earlier, because there is very little theory or evidence concerning the kinds of leader behavior required in various settings (Masoond et al., 2006), Table 1 proved to be very helpful in analyzing and categorizing the participants' comments. The characteristics listed in Table 1 are not all inclusive, and each leader's comments covered a different variation of the listed characteristics. However, within the variety, similarities emerged, such as cultural awareness, competence, and openness, concern for subordinates, ability to motivate others, mentoring of subordinates, facilitation of the free flow of information, and consideration of the consequences of his or her decisions (see Tables 9-16).

The leaders demonstrated that at their foundation they had knowledge of culture, which is thought to be the first place to start when seeking to become culturally intelligent (Thomas & Inkson, 2003). Each leader spoke about "creating" a certain organizational culture, which is as unique as the organizations in which they lead. Their comments about culture showed their understanding of the evolving nature of culture (Schein, 2004). According to their comments, the leaders facilitated cultural change by encouraging the free flow of information. The leaders showed an interest in and knowledge of dialogue. Their comments showed that they understood the importance of having generative and strategic dialogue. They did not use those technical words, but their comments regarding the importance of meeting regularly to share information and their explanation of how those meetings help when there has to be a decision about a specific issue points to the dialogic process. The overall theme concerning dialogue is that it is very important, and when having to choose between dialogue and the bottom line, it is seen as a "both/and" issue, not an "either/or" issue. These leaders admitted to being facilitators of dialogue; this is shown in the number of times their subordinates used the term *trustworthy* to describe their leaders. Ballantyne's (2004) assertion that dialogic interactions facilitate the development of trust and knowledge was seen in the experiences of these leaders and their subordinates.

The breakdown of the emergent themes supported me in answering the questions asked at the onset of this book.

Questions asked and answered. The overarching question for this book which fueled this journey towards understanding trans-cultural leadership was as follows: What are the experiences of trans-cultural leaders as they lead above and across the boundaries of culture? Green and Berthoud (2007) asserted that understanding diversity is a foundational skill that allows leaders to lead with relevance and effectiveness. Green and Berthoud's assertion is brought to life in the leaders' experiences involving being aware of the cultural differences of those who are under their leadership; for example, Rony provided a description of the diverseness of his subordinates and stated that his work is very multifaceted because it involves "doctors, scientists, engineers, and donor families."

This awareness came from being open to the various ideas and ways of doing business presented by those different from them in position and profession. These trans-cultural leaders sought to understand perspectives that allowed all those involved to understand each other's vantage point (Fontaine, 2007), as seen in Keith's description of his facilitation of conversations concerning resisting being taken over by large hospitals with people of many different practices and professions.

Maxwell (2006) asserted that leaders need to understand that people want to feel worthwhile, encouraged, and motivated, which aligns itself with Miller et al.'s (2000) list that includes sincere interest in subordinates as a characteristic of leadership that enhances the chances for success in working with diverse teams. Maxwell's and Miller et al.'s assertions were seen in the leaders' reliance on their ability to motivate others by showing their followers that they are really concerned with their well-being, as seen in Joe's belief that his job is to understand his subordinates and create opportunities for them to grow.

The leaders also provide room for their subordinates to think independently, which empowers their subordinates to perform at their best, as seen in Mark's assertion that Rony allows the experts in their fields be the experts.

All the leaders experienced and saw the importance of facilitating the free flow of information throughout their organizations, which increases a group's ability to learn collectively. Levine (1994) referred to this as "team dialogue" when he wrote,

> The core of team dialogue is collectively listening with spirit. That is: a group of people listens (individually) with selfless receptivity to each other's ideas, thereby emptying themselves to create a common vessel which—shaped by and sustained by the power of the group's collective listening—receives and contains a collective spirit. (p. 62)

The leaders' collective experiences showed that providing room for consistent communication created a common bond between people within the organization. This points to Bernstein's (1983) comment concerning Gadamer's analysis of dialogue and conversation, where such continual conversations created a common bond and a place where people can respect, listen, and be open to one another because such meetings allow people to test their opinions. And as Wheatley (2002) posited, consistent communication can be seen as the natural way people think together.

The leaders provide room for the sustained encounter between people within the organization. Buber's (1970) "I and You" relationship points to this type of encounter. The connection that occurs during the process of "Buberian turning" is what generates understanding, collaboration, and purposeful cooperative action. Interactions in multicultural organizations call for the genuine dialogue spoken of by Buber (1947/2002).

The leaders experienced the necessity of placing the needs of the group above their own needs, as seen in Keith's confession of always sacrificing for his colleagues. As listed in McGath, Arrow, and Berdahl's (1999) ways to lead diverse groups and impact the organizational environments, the leaders saw that leading in a multicultural environment called for them to be accommodating. D'Avirro (2007) posisted that giving back to the community is conducive to creating a positive busisness culture, which is akin to being community minded, and being community minded was a characteristic that all the leaders had when leading in an organization that reflects the communities in which they operate. Alma provided the clearest example of being community minded when describing her years of service by her and her organization in the communities she served.

The first subquestion, Does the leader have knowledge of his or her own culture, and how does that knowledge influence his or her decision-making process?, was seen in the leaders' answers to the qualifying questions and the first interview questions, which showed that each leader reported that they drew on his or her own cultural background when leading. They all appeared to take all of who they are to work with them, which connected to Swanson's (2004) assertion that in order to create an environment of cultural inclusiveness one must understand his or her own culture. From Joe's tough farm upbringing, which provided him with a strong work ethic, to Alma's experiences of religious witnessing with her grandmother, who exposed her to sharing ideas with people that may not agree, all leaders saw a connection to their cultural backgrounds.

The second subquestion asked how the leaders addressed issues of multiculturalism in their organizations. Each leader made a point to be culturally aware, competent, and open, which falls in the Heart, the Mind, and the Soul of trans-cultural leadership. Alma's belief that being respectful of everyone's cultural backgrounds, what their issues are, and what the interest are is very important is an example of the cultural awareness and openness needed in leading trans-culturally. Triandis (2003) noted that being culturally aware can help in generating understanding and communicating, and Green and Berthoud (2007) wrote, "Diversity awareness is a basic competency as demographics continue to change; diversity becomes ever more important for organizational development to increase its relevance and effectiveness" (p. 12). This research demonstrated that the leaders' relevance and effectiveness had at its core cultural competence and awareness, as seen in the 13 statements referring to culture by the leaders reflected in Table 9.

These leaders created an environment rooted in communication and dialogue, which allowed the people from differing cultures to interact frequently. They provided a space for the different organizational cultures within their organization to "turn to" each other and really see each other (Buber, 1970). The third subquestion, What has the trans-cultural leader done to move groups of different cultural backgrounds towards purposeful cooperative action?, springboards off the second subquestion, in that each leader attributed his or her ability to move the organization to open and free dialogue. Even though each leader saw dialogue's application marginally differently, they all expressed a belief that generative dialogue was essential to not only bring people with differences together but to generate purposeful cooperative action as well. The leaders influenced the dialogue's depth and width, which supports Hicks's (2008) assertion, "Whether people within an organization practice dialogue are largely determined by culture—company-wide, or within a department or division. The good news is that leadership can shape culture to encourage wider and deeper dialogue" (p. 17).

Two of the leaders indicated that generative dialogue actually helped in the decision-making process and the bottom line. They alluded to the idea that generative dialogue allows them to fluidly move into strategic dialogue mode and, thereby, help in the bottom line. Their allusion connects with Banathy and Jenlink's (2005) suggestion that "dialogue may be transformative or generative in nature, as well as strategic" (p. 5). Each leader voiced the importance of continuous connection through dialogue, as seen in several statements that pointed to the flow of information by the leaders in Table 9.

The fourth subquestion was, how does the transcultural leader handle resistance to different cultures uniting to perform a common goal or purpose? The leaders all attributed their willingness to continue to communicate and dialogue with those who resist understanding more fully the scope and importance of the directional shift of their organization. Overcoming the hurdle of resistance was tied to the leaders' ideas concerning the dialogic process and was directly related to the cultures they created. As stated earlier, Coffey and Tombari (2005) posited the need to identify and eliminate hurdles that arise during the process of creating diverse organizational cultures. The leader must commit to continuous learning and improvement and promote communication and education. Each leader admitted that there comes a time when movement must happen with or without those who resist. On those occasions, if the final decision is the up to the leaders, they will proceed with the hopes of subsequent agreement.

The answers provided above show the complexities of leading trans-culturally. A trans-cultural leader must be able to draw on all aspects of himself or herself in order to transcend the boundaries that separate cultures. The leader must rely on being what connects them all, which is his or her humanity, whether it is in the organization or community. Such leaders must be transparent enough to walk in the humanness of their existence by being relational and even funny at times.

Implications of this book. This book provides the reader with a "snapshot" in time of the experiences of four trans-cultural leaders from various fields as they lead people of different races, genders, professions, and/or disciplines towards purposeful cooperative action. This work gives insight into the best practices of those leaders and shows the aspects that are common to these four leaders and potentially to all those who endeavor to lead people with differences toward purposeful cooperative action. This research also shows that in order to lead effectively in this century, one must have an understanding of culture and an ability to facilitate dialogue in a fashion that promotes inclusion.

I have learned that leading trans-culturally calls on leaders to be very aware of their beliefs and actions and to undertake their work consciously. Trans-cultural leadership is a way of being rather than a strategy. To develop a trans-cultural mindset, one has to be dedicated to being ever curious and willing, as Buber (1970) proposed to "turn toward the other" and embrace relationships of care that support continuous learning and development.

Conclusion

This book provides the leader who leads in multicultural environments with a snapshot of the experiences of four trans-cultural leaders from different fields as they lead people with many differences towards purposeful cooperative action. It is my hope that this book will help leaders become trans-cultural in their approach to leadership by tapping into the Heart, the Mind, and the Soul of trans-cultural leadership. Such a leader will be able to facilitate the coming together of diverse people within organizations and communities in order to carry out a common purpose. I trust that this book will increase the awareness of leaders concerning the innate strength of cultural inclusion as it applies to originations and communities. Cultural inclusion moves away from the "melting pot" mentality towards the "patchwork quilt" way of bringing people and groups together by encouraging the continuation of what makes the person or group unique while facilitating true Buberian (1970) "turning towards" each other—turning that produces connection, collaboration, and action.

This book has taken me on a journey much like the one spoken of in Campbell's (1990) work. Whereas this journey started as a result of my embarking on my "life's call" to service, it took me to a place that my friends, my family, and my peers could not truly understand. This journey presented several trials and victories, but, in the end, I developed an appreciation of leaders who lead trans-culturally. This type of leader must be able to transcend the boundaries of culture in order for him or her to "move from the realm of visions and dreams, of ideas, to the land of human needs, conflicts, and limitations" (Stech, 2009, p. 21) The completion of this book is only the beginning of my journey towards understanding the concepts of leading in multicultural environments and the power of dialogue.

About the Author

Dr. Jonathan E. Smith has a range of administrative and management experiences beginning at the company and battalion levels of the personnel offices in the US Marine Corps. He has led others as a supervisor, director, and president and CEO of JES Connections through Counseling, Consulting and Coaching. Dr. Smith honed his leadership skills by working several years in the crisis intervention and stabilization field in California and Virginia. Dr. Smith's experiences and knowledge equip him to help others as a marriage and family therapist, minister, coach, and consultant, and allow him to facilitate positive change in people's lives. It is Dr. Smith's life purpose to help people maximize their relationship with God and each other at home, church, and the workplace.

Jonathan has been married to his wife, Katara, for twenty-five years. They have four children, Dakari, Imani, Joshua, and Niyah. The Smith family lives in Virginia Beach, Virginia, where Katara is a middle school teacher and Jonathan pursues his life's purpose of serving others as a clinical supervisor, licensed marriage and family therapist, consultant, coach, and ordained minister.

References

Ballantyne, D. (2004). Dialogue and its role in the development of relationship specific knowledge. *Journal of Business & Industrial Marketing, 19*(2), 114-123.

Banathy, B. H. (1992). *A Systems View of Education Concepts ant Principles for Effective Practice*. Englewood Cliffs, NJ: Educational Technology Publications, Inc.

Banathy, B. H., & Jenlink, P. M. (2005). Dialogue conversation as culture creating and consciousness evolving. In B. H. Banathy & P. M. Jenlink (Eds.), *Dialogue as a means of collective communication* (pp. 3-14). New York, NY: Kluwer Academic/Plenum.

Bass, B. M. (1998). The ethics of transformational leadership. In J. Ciulla (Ed.), *Ethics, the heart of leadership* (pp. 169-189). Westport, CT: Praeger.

Bell, M. (1996). Case study dialogue in the public sector. *Management Development Review, 9*(3), 20-21.

Bernstein, R. (1983). *Beyond objectivism and relativism science, hermeneutics, and praxis*. Philadelphia, PA: University of Pennsylvania Press.

Bohm, D. (1996). *Bohm on dialogue*. New York, NY: Routledge Classics.

Bokeno, R. M. (2007). Dialogue at work? What it is and isn't. *Development and Learning in Organizations, 21*(1), 9-11.

Bond, M. (2003). Cross-cultural social psychology and the real world of culturally diverse teams and dyads. In D. Tjosvold & K. Leung (Eds.), *Cross-cultural management* (pp. 43-58). Burlington, VT: Ashgate.

Brown, J. F. (2007). *The global business leader, practical advice for success in a transcultural marketplace*. New York, NY: Palgrave Macmillan.

Brown, T. (2005). *Corporate integrity*. New York, NY: Cambridge University Press.

Buber, M. (1970). *I and thou* (W. Kaufmann, Trans.). New York, NY: Simon & Schuster.

Buber, M. (2002). *Between man and man*. New York, NY: Routledge Classics. (Original work published 1947)

Burns, J. M. (1978). *Leadership*. New York, NY: Harper and Row.

Caley, N. (2007). Including all points of view. *Nation's Restaurant News, 41*(5), 84.

Campbell, J. (1990). *The hero with a thousand faces*. Princeton, NJ: University of Princeton Press.

Christie, P. M., Kwon, I., Stoeberl, P., & Baumhart, R. (2003). A cross-cultural comparison of ethical attitudes of business managers: India, Korea, and the United States. *Journal of Business Ethics, 46*(3), 263-282. Retrieved November 12, 2007, from ProQuest database.

Ciulla, J. B. (Ed.). (1998). *Ethics, the heart of leadership*. Westport, CT: Praeger.

Coffey, C., & Tombari, N. (2005, July/August). The bottom-line for work/life leadership: Linking diversity and organizational culture. *Ivey Business Journal, 69*(6), 1-6.

Corey, G. (1996). *Theory and practice of counseling and psychotherapy* (5th ed.). New York, NY: Brooks/Cole.

D'Avirro, M. (2007). Employee benefits & HR. In *Create a Positive Business Culture*. Retrieved November 13, 2007, from http://www.cnybj.com/Default.aspx.

Fontaine, R. (2007). Cross-cultural management: Six perspectives. *Cross-Cultural Management, 14*(2), 125-135.

Gandz, J. (2007). Great leadership is good leadership. *Ivey Business Journal, 71*(5), 1-7.

Green, R. D., & Berthoud, H. (2007). OD is diversity: Differences are at the heart of the field. *OD Practitioner, 39*(2), 9-12.

Grillo, L. (2005). Diversity is an action verb. *Issues in Higher Education, 22*(21), 45.

Hall, T. E. (1989). *Beyond culture.* New York, NY: Anchor Books. (Original work published 1977)

Hamel, G. (2007). *The future of management.* Boston, MA: Harvard Business School.

Hargrove, R. (2003). *Masterful coaching* (Rev. ed.). San Francisco, CA: Jossey-Bass/Pfeiffer.

Hicks, D. (2008). Rediscovering the lost art of dialogue. *Rough Notes, 151*(2), 16-17.

Hill, L. (1992). Becoming a manager—the challenge of exercising authority. *Black Enterprise, 23*(5), 131-140.

Hoffman, D., & Hendrickson, A. (2006). Driving diversity in the boardroom. *Chief Executive, 222*, 43-46.

Hofstede, G. (2003). The universal and the specific in 21st century management. In D. Tjosvold & K.

Leung (Eds.), *Cross-cultural management* (pp. 29-42). Burlington, VT: Ashgate.

Hofstede, G., & Hofstede, G. J. (2005). *Cultures and organizations: Software of the mind* (2nd ed.). New York, NY: McGraw-Hill.

Isaacs, W. (1999). *Dialogue and the art of thinking togeather.* New York, NY: Currency and Doubleday.

Kane-Urrabazo, C. (2006). Management's role in shaping organizational culture. *Journal of Nursing Management, 14,* 188-194.

Katz, J., & Miller, F. (2007). The next leap forward: Diversity and inclusion—an OD opportunity. *OD Practitioner, 39*(2), 4-8.

Keeley, M. (1998). The trouble with tranformational leadership: Toward a federalist ethic for organizations. In J. Ciulla (Ed.), *Ethics, the heart of leadership* (pp. 111-144). Westpoit, CT: Praeger.

Kersten, A. (2000). Diversity management, dialogue, dialects and diversion. *Journal of Organizational Change Management, 13*(3), 235-248.

King, M. L. (1986). The ethical demands for intergration. In J. M. Washington (Ed.), *A testament of hope, the essential writings of Martin Luther King, Jr.*

(pp. 117-125). New York, NY: Harper & Row. (Original work published 1963)

Klie, S. (2007). Lots of talk, not much action on diversity. *Canadian HR Reporter, 20*(1), 9.

Kramer, K. (2003). *Martin Buber's I and thou practicing living dialogue*. Mahwah, NJ: Paulist Press.

Levine, L. (1994). Listening with spirit and the art of team dialogue. *Journal of Organizational Change Management, 7*(1), 61-73

Lewis, R. D. (2006). *When cultures colide: Leading across cultures* (3rd ed.). Boston, MA: Nicholas Brealey. (Original work published 1996)

McGath, J, Arrow, H., & Berdahl, J. (1999). Cooperation and conflict as manifestations of coordination in small groups. *Polish Psychological Bulletin, 30*, 1-14.

March, J. G., & Olsen, J. P. (1976). *Ambiguity and choice in organizations*. Bergen, Norway: Universitetsforlaget.

Maslow, A. H. (1943). A theory of human motivation. *Psychological Review, 50*, 370-396.

Masoond, S. A., Dani, S. S., Burns, N. D., & Backhouse, C. J. (2006). Transformtional leadership and organizational culture: The situational strength perspective. *Wolfson School of Mechanical and Manufacturing Engineering, 220*, 941-949.

Maxwell, J. C. (2005). *The 360° leader: Developing your influence from anywhere in the organization*. Nashville, TN: Thomas Nelson.

Maxwell, J. C. (2006). Lead others by learning to lead yourself. *Your Business at Home*, 115-117.

Miller, D., Fields, R., Kumar, A., & Ortiz, R. (2000, November/December). Leadership and organizational vision in managing a multiethnic and multicultural project team. *Journal of Management in Engineering*, 18-22.

Murray, H. A. (1938). *Explorations in Personality*. New York, NY: Oxford University Press.

Negandhi, A. R. (1983). Cross-cultural management research: Trend and future directions. *Jounal of International Business Studies, 14*(000002), 17-28.

Newman, B., & Newman, P. (1999). *Development through life: A psychosocial approach* (7th ed.). Belmont, CA: Wadsworth. (Original work published 1975)

Nieto, S. (2000). *Affirming diversity: The sociopolitical context of multicultural education* (3rd ed.). New York, NY: Addison Wesley Longman.

Obama, B. (2009). *Text of President Barack Obama's inaugural address*. Retrieved January 23, 2009 from http://news.yahoo.com/s/ap/20090120/_ap_on_go_pr_wh/inauguration_obama_text/print

Oswick, C., Anthony, P., Keenoy, T., Mangham, I, & Grant, D. (2000). A dialogic analysis of organizational learning. *Journal of Management Studies, 37*, 888-901.

Peterson, B. (2004). *Cultural intelligence, a guide to working with people from other cultures*. Boston, MA: Intercultural Press.

Resick, C. J., Hanges, P. J., Dickson, M. W., & Mitchelson, J. K. (2006). A cross-cultural examination of the endorsement of ethical leadership. *Journal of Business Ethics, 63*, 345-359.

Schein, E. H. (1996). Three cultures of management: The key to organizational learing. *Sloan Management Review, 38*(1), 9-20.

Schein, E. H. (2004). *Organizational culture and leadership* (3rd ed.). San Francisco, CA: Jossey-Bass.

Seijts, G., & Kilgour, D. (2007). Principled leadership: Taking the hard right. *Ivey Business Journal, 71*(5), 8-17.

Senge, P. M. (1990). *The fifth discipline*. New York, NY: Currency Doubleday.

Senge, P., Kleiner, A., Roberts, C., Ross, R., & Smith, B. (1994). *The fifth discipline fieldbook*. New York, NY: Currency Doubleday.

Simons, G. F., Vázquez, C., Harris, P. H. (1993). *Transcultural Leadership: Empowering the diverse workforce.* Houston, TX: Gulf.

Smith, J. E. (2006, July). *The appreciative church—Relationships with God, self, and others; The key to a healthy, well-balanced multicultural and multiracial community of faith.* Unpublished manuscript, Saybrook University, San Francisco, CA.

Smith, J. E. (2008, November). *Leading across human barriers: The many to one purpose.* Unpublished manuscript, Saybrook University, San Francisco, CA.

Smith, J.E. (2010). *Trans-Cultural Leadership and the Creation of Inclusive Organizations that Support Cooperative Action.* Doctoral dissertation, Saybrook University.

Solomon, R. (1998). Ethical leadership emotions and trust: Beyond "charisma." In J. Ciulla (Ed.), *Ethics: The heart of leadership* (pp. 87-107). Westport, CT: Praeger.

Stech, E. L. (2009). A trans-cultural perspective on leadership and leader development. *Leadership Review, 9,* 20-27.

Sue, D. W., & Sue, D. (2003). *Counseling the culturally diverse: Theory and practice* (4th ed.). New York, NY: John Wiley.

Swanson, J. (2004). Diversity: Creating an enviornment of inclusiveness. *Nursing Administration Quarterly, 28*(3), 207-211.

Thomas, D. C., & Inkson, K. (2003). *Cultural intelligence*. San Francisco, CA: Berrett-Koehler.

Triandis, H. (2003). Forty-five years of researching the culture and behavior link: An intellectual autobiography. In D. Tjosvold & K. Leung (Eds.), *Cross-cultural management* (pp. 11-27). Burlington, VT: Ashgate.

Triandis, H. (2006). Cultural intelligence in organizatons. *Group & Organizational Management, 31*(1), 20-26.

Trompenaars, F., & Hampden-Turner, C. (2001). *21 leaders for the 21st century*. Oxford, England: Capstone.

Trompenaars, F., & Hampden-Turner, C. (2004). *Managing people across cultures*. West Sussex, England: Capstone.

Varney, J. (1996). Techniques the power of dialogue. *Management Development Review, 9*(2), 30-32.

Vine, W. E., Unger, M. F., & White, W. (Eds.). (1985). *Vine's complete expository dictionary of old and new testament words* (2nd ed.). Nashville, TN: Thomas Nelson. (Original work published 1980)

Whitney, D., & Trosten-Bloom, A. (2003). *The power of appreciative inquiry*. San Francisco, CA: Berrett-Koehler.

Wheatley, M. J. (2002). *Turning to one another*. San Francisco, CA: Berrett-Koehler.

Williams, L. W. (2007). How culture evolves: An institutional analysis. *International Journal of Social Economics, 34*(4), 249-267.

Wubbolding, R. E. (1988). *Using reality therapy*. New York, NY: Harper & Row.

Yankelovich, D. (1999). *The magic of dialogue transforming conflict into cooperation*. New York, NY: Touchstone.

Zodhiates, S. (1994). *The complete word study Old Testament*. Chattanooga, TN: AMG.

www.ingramcontent.com/pod-product-compliance
Lightning Source LLC
Chambersburg PA
CBHW032017170526
45157CB00002B/732